ORIGINS OF DISOBEDIENCE

CREATION, REBELLION

AND GODS' PLAN FOR RESTORATION

Published By:

Michael McCullough

Copyright © 2024 All rights reserved.

This book, or any portion thereof, may not be reproduced, distributed, or transmitted in any form or by any means without the express written consent of the copyright holder, except for brief quotations in book reviews and certain other noncommercial uses permitted by copyright law.

Table of Contents

Introduction to Section 1 / Creation	1
Chapter 1 - The Eternal God:	3
Chapter 2 - The Divine Blueprint:	7
Chapter 3 - The Heavens:	13
Chapter 4 - Unveiling the Spiritual Realm	19
Chapter 5 - In His Image:	27
Chapter 6 – Eden:	33
Introduction to Section 2 / "Rebellion"	37
Chapter 7 - The Bright Star:	41
Chapter 8 – The Two Falls:	45
Chapter 9 - The Ancient Foe:	51
Chapter 10 - Choice and Consequence:	55
Chapter 11 - The Ripple Effect:	61
Chapter 12 - The Heavenly Rebellion:	65
Chapter 13 - Giants Among Us:	71
Chapter 14 - Waters of Judgment:	77
Chapter 15 - After the Waters:	83
Chapter 16 - Reaching for Heaven:	89

Chapter 17 - Divided Lands:	95
Introduction to Section 3 / "Restoration"	101
Chapter 18 – Abraham's Covenant:	103
Chapter 19 - The Legacy of Promise:	109
Chapter 20 - Establishing a Holy Nation	117
Chapter 21 - Conquering Canaan:	123
Chapter 22 - A Bridge to Kingship:	129
Chapter 23 - The Davidic Covenant:	135
Chapter 24 - The Road to Restoration:	141
Chapter 25 - The Prophets:	149
Chapter 26 - The Coming of the Messiah:	155
Chapter 27 - The Great Commission:	161
Chapter 28 – From Judgement to Glory:	169
Chapter 29 - Restoration Complete:	175

Introduction to Section 1 / Creation

From the dawn of human thought, we have been irresistibly drawn to life's most profound mysteries: Who is God? Why do we exist? What lies beyond the world we can see? For millennia, these questions have captivated our souls, urging us to look beyond the material world and search for truths that seem just out of reach. This work is an invitation—not just to observe, but to actively explore these eternal questions. Together, we'll embark on a journey of reflection, stepping beyond the familiar and into the heart of the divine unknown.

We begin by contemplating the nature of God Himself—an attempt to grasp the unfathomable. What does it mean to know a God who is eternal, existing beyond time's relentless flow? Imagine standing on the shore of a vast ocean, waves rolling and retreating with each passing moment. These waves are like time, constantly in motion. But God is like the boundless depths beneath, untouched by the surface, unmoved by the passing of hours, days, and years. His being transcends what we can see and feel, extending into an eternity that escapes human comprehension.

Can we, as finite beings, truly understand the infinite? What does it mean for our lives that God exists beyond time, and yet, intimately engages with His creation? These are not merely abstract thoughts—they shape the very core of our reality. In this exploration, we seek to glimpse how God's eternal nature impacts the world we inhabit, the stars above us, and even our own hearts.

From this reflection on God's nature, we turn to the act of creation itself. In the vastness of His eternity, why did God choose to bring the universe into being? As we gaze at the night sky, dotted with countless stars, we might wonder: Is creation simply an expression of divine power, or does it also reflect divine love? In the intricate harmony of the cosmos, in the laws that govern stars and planets, we see glimpses of something greater. Could the universe be more than just a physical reality? Could it be a reflection of God's intent, each element part of a grander design that speaks to a deeper purpose?

As our journey deepens, we look beyond the stars to the spiritual realms and encounter the Elohim—mysterious, powerful beings who dwell within God's heavenly domain. Who are they, and what role do they play in the governance of creation? Their existence invites us to consider the layers of divine order, where cosmic forces act as agents of the Creator's will. Through them, we see a reflection of God's authority, purpose, and glory, challenging our understanding of the divine hierarchy.

Finally, we turn our gaze back to Earth, to humanity—the crowning creation, made in God's own image. What does it mean to bear the divine likeness? Just as an imperfect mirror reflects light, so too do we reflect God's nature, even in our imperfections. How does this divine imprint shape our purpose in the grand narrative of existence? To bear His image is not merely to exist, but to shine with His likeness, infusing His presence into the world around us.

Next, we will step into Eden—a paradise where heaven and earth once coexisted in perfect harmony, where creation was as it was meant to be. And as our exploration ascends through the celestial realms, we will encounter one of God's highest beings: Lucifer, who fell from the heights of glory. But that is a story for the next chapter, where we will explore the cosmic drama of rebellion and its consequences.

For now, we begin at the beginning—before time, before creation itself—with a God who is eternal.

Chapter 1 - The Eternal God: Revealing His Divine Nature

Think back to one of your earliest memories. Perhaps it's the thrill of riding a bike for the first time, your feet wobbling as you seek balance, followed by the rush of your first successful pedal. Or maybe it's your first day of school, filled with both excitement and nerves. These memories feel distant, as if they belong to another time entirely—moments tucked away in the far corners of your mind.

Now, stretch your imagination further. Picture time as a long road winding behind you, extending far beyond the limits of your personal experience. Move past the decades and centuries of recorded history—through the bustling streets of ancient Rome, the rise of empires, the words of prophets and poets. Keep going, past all of human civilization, until you reach the profound opening words of Scripture: "In the beginning, God created the heavens and the earth" (Genesis 1:1).

But what about before that? What existed before the universe, before the first ray of light pierced the darkness? This is where our understanding falters, for before Genesis 1:1, there was no time. No matter. Only God.

Here, we encounter one of the most profound mysteries of faith: God's eternity. Unlike us, who are bound by time—moving from one moment to the next—God exists outside of time. He is not confined by the ticking of the clock. Psalm 90:2 declares, "Before the mountains were brought forth, or ever you had formed the earth and the world, from everlasting to everlasting, you are God." He is the same yesterday, today, and forever, existing in a way that escapes our ability to fully comprehend.

This reality might make our heads spin. After all, aspects of God such as His love or justice are easier for us to grasp because we experience them, at least in part, within the confines of time. But His eternal nature? His existence beyond time's boundaries? That stretches our understanding in ways that can be difficult to relate to.

Yet, instead of being frustrated by what we cannot fully comprehend, we should let this truth fill us with awe. God's eternal nature magnifies His greatness and reveals just how vastly different He is from anything we know. He is constant, unchanging, and limitless, standing outside the flow of time while being fully present within every moment of it.

The Practical Impact of God's Eternity

But what does this mean for us, bound as we are by time? Why should God's eternal nature matter to our daily lives?

First, it assures us that God is unchanging. While everything around us shifts—seasons, circumstances, people—God remains the same. Hebrews 13:8 reminds us, "Jesus Christ is the same yesterday and today and forever." His promises endure because they are rooted in His eternal character. His love, grace, and justice do not waver with time; they are as constant as He is.

This truth gives us peace. In a world marked by uncertainty, where the future often feels unpredictable, we can rest in the certainty that God, who existed before time began, holds all of history in His hands. Nothing surprises Him, nothing escapes His attention, and nothing is beyond His reach.

God's Eternal Attributes: Omniscience, Omnipotence, and Omnipresence

God's eternal nature also shapes how we understand His other attributes. Because He exists beyond time, He is omniscient—He knows all things, past, present, and future. Isaiah 46:10 declares, "Declaring the end from the beginning and from ancient times things not yet done." Nothing is hidden from Him; no event or decision falls outside His knowledge.

Likewise, His eternal nature undergirds His omnipotence. He is not constrained by the limitations of time or space. As Genesis 18:14 reminds us, "Is anything too hard for the LORD?" His power does not diminish with time, and nothing decays or weakens His strength.

Finally, God is omnipresent—everywhere at once, at all times. Psalm 139:7 asks, "Where shall I go from your Spirit? Or where shall I flee from your presence?" No matter where we find ourselves in time or space, God is already there, fully present. His eternal nature allows Him to be intimately involved in each of our lives, always present, always near.

From Eternity to the Trinity: A Divine Relationship

As we reflect on the eternal nature of God, we come to a profound realization: God's eternity is not solitary. The God who transcends time exists in a relationship within Himself—as Father, Son, and Holy Spirit. This divine relationship is central to understanding God's nature, especially in His role as Creator.

In Genesis 1:1, we see the Father initiating creation, speaking the universe into existence. But in the very next verse, we find the Spirit of God hovering over the waters, actively involved in shaping the world. And the New Testament reveals the role of the Son, the eternal Word, through whom all things were made. John 1:1-3 declares, "In the beginning was the Word, and the Word was with God, and the Word was God. He was in the beginning with God. All things were made through Him, and without Him was not anything made that was made."

The creation of the universe is the cooperative work of the triune God. The Father wills it, the Son enacts it, and the Spirit breathes life into it.

his act of creation is a reflection of the relational nature of God—eternal, yet always moving toward relationship.

Conclusion: The Relevance of Eternity

As we close this chapter, consider the majesty of a God who exists beyond time and yet chooses to step into time. This eternal God invites us to trust in His unchanging character, to rest in the knowledge that He holds the past, present, and future in His hands. His eternal nature is not distant or detached; it is deeply personal, as He walks with us through every moment of our lives.

In the next chapter, we'll explore why the eternal God chose to create us, how His plan for humanity unfolds through time, and the purpose He has woven into the fabric of creation—a purpose that extends into eternity itself.

Chapter 2 - The Divine Blueprint: God's Choice to Create

Why Did God Create Everything?

In the previous chapter, we marveled at God's eternal nature—His existence beyond time, with no beginning and no end. It's an awe-inspiring thought: a God who is infinite, self-sufficient, and lacking nothing. And yet, that leaves us with a question: If God is complete in Himself, what moved Him to create the universe, the earth, and ultimately, us? What could possibly motivate a perfect, eternal being to bring all of creation into existence?

Was it loneliness? A desire for companionship? Or is there something far more profound at play? To understand this mystery, we need to dive deeper into who God is—His character, His purpose, and the immense depth of His love.

Let's journey through this together.

Creation: An Overflow of God's Love and Glory

When you gaze up at the stars on a clear night or feel the warmth of a sunset wash over you, it's easy to be filled with a sense of awe. Creation's beauty and majesty seem to stir something deep within us. But behind all that beauty lies something even more profound: God's love.

And this love isn't distant or abstract—it's deeply personal. At the heart of everything God does is the truth that God is love. As 1 John 4:8 tells us, "God is love." Not just loving, not just filled with affection, but love itself. Every action He takes, every decision He makes, flows from this core reality.

Pause and think about this for a moment: The universe exists because of love. Creation is not an act born of need or lack but an expression of God's generous, overflowing love. His nature is inherently creative, and this creativity is fueled by a desire to share His goodness. Before time began, God existed as Father, Son, and Holy Spirit in perfect, harmonious relationship. Out of this love, He created—not because He was lonely or incomplete, but because His love is so abundant that it reaches out, shares, and multiplies.

Isaiah 43:7 reminds us, "Everyone who is called by my name, whom I created for my glory." Everything—every star, every mountain, every heartbeat—exists to reflect His glory. And you, too, were uniquely created as a reflection of His deep, personal love.

Let this sink in: You were not only created out of love but for love. Your very existence is a response to God's desire to express His glory and invite you into His infinite love.

A Display of God's Infinite Power and Wisdom

Creation isn't just beautiful—it's purposeful. Have you ever stood beneath a sky full of stars or sat quietly by the ocean and felt something stir deep inside you? That sense of wonder is more than just admiration for nature's grandeur—it's your soul recognizing the fingerprints of its Creator. Psalm 19:1 says, "The heavens declare the glory of God, and the sky above proclaims His handiwork."

Every part of creation, from the smallest atom to the largest galaxy, not only reflects God's love but reveals His infinite power and wisdom. The delicate balance of ecosystems, the fine-tuned laws of physics, the astonishing complexity of life—all point to a Creator who is both infinitely powerful and profoundly wise.

Romans 1:20 reminds us, "For since the creation of the world, God's invisible qualities—His eternal power and divine nature—have been clearly seen, being understood from what has been made." The vastness of the universe declares His greatness, while the details of a single flower reflect His attention to the smallest things. Creation tells us not only that God is powerful but that His power is wielded with wisdom and care.

As you marvel at creation's beauty, know this: it is an invitation to know the One who made it. The universe sings a song that points us back to the Creator, and it beckons us to enter into a deeper relationship with Him.

God's Desire for Relationship

Here's where it becomes even more personal. Creation isn't just a display of God's glory, like a masterpiece hung in a gallery to be admired from a distance. It's far more intimate than that. God, who existed in perfect harmony within Himself—Father, Son, and Holy Spirit—created with a specific purpose: relationship.

Think about Genesis 1:26, where God says, "Let us make man in our image, after our likeness." Out of everything God created—the galaxies, oceans, animals, and plants—only humanity was made in His image. This is no small thing. You and I were uniquely crafted to reflect God's nature, not just in what we do but in the very essence of who we are.

Being made in God's image means we were designed for relationship—with Him and with each other. This is the heart of creation: God's desire for us to be His, to live in His love, and to walk in intimate fellowship with Him. As Psalm 100:3 beautifully says, "It is He who made us, and we are His." We are not distant observers of God's work; we are invited participants in His grand design.

Imagine that for a moment: The same God who shaped the stars wants to know you, personally and intimately. He created you not just to exist, but to live in a loving relationship with Him, reflecting His love to the world around you.

What does this mean for us? It means that every day is an opportunity to draw closer to the One who made us. It means living a life that reflects His nature—loving, giving, creating, and growing in faith. We weren't just created to be; we were created to be with Him, walking alongside our Creator in a relationship of love and trust.

Creation with Purpose: A Grand Design

Nothing God does is random. There is no chaos in His plan. Every star in the sky, every leaf on a tree, every breath you take—all of it is part of a grand design. Ephesians 1:11 tells us that God works "all things according to the counsel of His will." Nothing in the universe is accidental. Every part of creation, including your life, has meaning and purpose.

Here's where it gets deeply personal: You are not an accident. Your life has purpose, and it is woven into the fabric of God's greater plan. Ephesians 2:10 says we are God's workmanship, "created in Christ Jesus for good works." Just as creation reflects God's glory, your life is meant to reflect His love and His purpose.

You were created with intention, formed by the hand of the Creator who knows every detail of your existence. And this purpose is not limited to what you accomplish but extends to who you are. You are part of God's grand design, and your role in that design is essential.

Creation as Part of God's Redemptive Plan

What's truly amazing is that God created knowing what would come next. Before He ever said, "Let there be light," He knew humanity would fall. He knew sin would enter the world, and that creation would be marred by suffering. But He created anyway, because His plan from the very beginning wasn't just to create—it was to redeem.

Ephesians 1:4-5 tells us that before the foundation of the world, God chose us in Christ, predestining us for adoption as sons and daughters. Creation, therefore, is not only an expression of God's power but also the backdrop for His plan of redemption. The beauty of creation reflects His glory, but the cross reflects His grace. Both are central to His divine plan.

God knew that in creating us, we would one day fall into sin and be in need of salvation. Yet, He chose to create anyway because He already had a plan to redeem us through Christ. This shows us something incredible about God's nature: His love is not deterred by our failures. His creative power is intertwined with His redemptive purpose, and this gives creation itself profound meaning. Every sunrise, every heartbeat, exists within a divine plan that moves toward restoration.

A Glimpse into the Heavenly Realms

In this chapter, we've uncovered how creation mirrors God's love, power, and desire for relationship. But there is more. Creation is not limited to the physical world we see. Beyond what our eyes can perceive, there are heavenly realms—mysterious, vast, and filled with purpose beyond human understanding.

As we continue our journey, we'll explore the significance of these realms, the structure of the three heavens, and how they fit into God's grand design. Together, we'll peel back the layers of creation and uncover even more about His eternal plan.

Let's step forward into this awe-inspiring exploration, for God's design stretches far beyond our earthly experience, inviting us to discover the depths of His love and purpose that reach into eternity.

Jeremiah 32:17

Ah, Lord God! It is you who have made the heavens and the earth by your great power and by your outstretched arm! Nothing is too hard for you

Chapter 3 - The Heavens:
Exploring the Realms of God's Creation

"In the beginning, God created the heavens and the earth."
Genesis 1:1

As we explored in the previous chapter, God's creation is an overflow of His love, a reflection of His power, and a key part of His grand design for redemption. But God's act of creation didn't stop with the earth—it extends far beyond, into realms both seen and unseen.

From the very first verse of the Bible, we are introduced to the majesty of God's creation: the heavens, the earth, and every detail in between. The use of "heavens" in the plural invites us to explore something deeper than just the sky above. It points to layers of creation, each with its own purpose and meaning.

God's creation of the heavens is not a vague concept. Each realm is rich with beauty, order, and intentionality, revealing different aspects of His character and desire for a relationship with us. So, let's take a journey through these realms—the threefold heavens that God designed with purpose. From the skies we see every day to the very throne room of God, each level tells a story—a story that reveals who God is and what He desires for His creation, including you.

The First Heaven: The Skies We Know

Let's begin with the first heaven—the one we experience every day. Step outside and look up at the vast, open sky. Picture it: the endless blue where clouds float, birds soar, and the sun rises faithfully each morning. It's familiar, yet there's something magnificent about it. The beauty, the rhythm, the way it cradles our world—all speak to something greater.

When God created this first heaven, it wasn't just to give us something beautiful to look at or a backdrop for the weather. He designed it with deep purpose, as a constant reminder of His provision, creativity, and presence. Every sunrise is His handiwork. Every drop of rain is a gift of His care. Genesis 1:6-8 reminds us that God separated the waters to form the heavens, creating a space where life could thrive.

But the sky does more than sustain life—it speaks to us. "The heavens declare the glory of God, and the sky above proclaims His handiwork," says Psalm 19:1. Have you ever stood beneath a sky full of stars or watched a sunset and felt a sense of wonder, as though creation itself was urging you to look beyond what you can see? Those moments are not coincidences. God designed the first heaven to be a living testimony of His glory.

Why was the first heaven created? It was created for life—yours, mine, and every living creature on earth. It's a canvas for God's ongoing creation, where His artistry is displayed every day. But more than that, it draws our eyes upward. It invites us to remember that there is more to life than what we can touch and see—that we are part of a larger story unfolding under the watchful eye of the Creator.

The skies may feel like a ceiling to this world, but they are also a window into something deeper. They remind us that, while we are bound to this earth for now, there's a greater reality beyond. Every time you look up, remember: God is there, sustaining it all. He invites you to see His fingerprints in everything—from the simplest cloud to the most breathtaking sunset.

The Second Heaven: The Realm Beyond

But the heavens don't end with the skies we see each day. Beyond the clouds and the open blue is a deeper realm—a vast expanse filled with stars and mysteries far beyond what we can fully grasp. This is the second heaven, where the night sky stretches out in endless beauty and complexity. When you step outside on a clear, starry night and see millions of stars scattered across the sky, you are witnessing a glimpse of this second heaven.

There's a reason you feel so small under that vast expanse—it's intentional. God designed the heavens, particularly what we call the "second heaven," not only to inspire awe but to remind us of His majesty, power, and the order of His creation. In Genesis 1:14-18, we see God's purpose in creating the second heaven: "Let there be lights in the expanse of the heavens to separate the day from the night. And let them be for signs and for seasons, and for days and years... to give light upon the earth." The sun, moon, and stars serve practical purposes—guiding us, marking time—but beyond that, they point to a deeper truth.

The second heaven reveals God's sovereignty. Every star, every planet, every galaxy is perfectly placed by His hand. The vastness of the universe humbles us, reminding us of a design far beyond what we can see with our eyes. But the second heaven is not just a place of beauty; it's also a realm of spiritual conflict.

Scripture gives us glimpses of this. In Daniel 10:12-13, an angel sent to deliver a message to Daniel was delayed for 21 days due to spiritual warfare in the heavens. This battle took place in the second heaven—a battleground where angelic beings and demonic forces war over the fate of humanity. Ephesians 6:12 reinforces this idea, reminding us that "we do not wrestle against flesh and blood, but against rulers, against authorities, against cosmic powers over this present darkness, against spiritual forces of evil in the heavenly places."

Though we may not see it, we often feel the effects of this unseen battle in our own lives. Whether it's through personal struggles, challenges in our relationships, or moments of doubt, we are constantly reminded that there is more going on beyond what we can see. Yet, through it all, God's sovereignty remains unquestioned, and His purpose will prevail.

Why does the second heaven exist? It displays God's glory in the vastness of creation, but it also reminds us that there is a spiritual battle raging beyond what we can see. It's a realm where forces of good and evil contend, where God's will is being enacted, and His victory is assured. We may feel the weight of these battles in our daily lives, but we can rest in the truth that God remains in control, and His purpose will not be thwarted.

As you reflect on the second heaven, remember that it shows us both the beauty of God's creation and the reality of spiritual warfare. The battles we face are not merely physical—they have roots in the spiritual realm. But take heart: God is sovereign over all, and His plan for you will not fail.

The Third Heaven: Where God's Glory Dwells

Now, let's step beyond what our eyes can see into something truly extraordinary—the third heaven. This is not just a far-off concept or an abstract idea. The third heaven is a real place, and it is where God Himself dwells. When the apostle Paul speaks of being "caught up to the third heaven" in 2 Corinthians 12:2, he gives us a glimpse into a realm of unimaginable beauty, holiness, and perfection—the very throne room of God.

This third heaven exists right now. It is where God reigns, overseeing everything we know and see, as well as everything we cannot. It is not just the seat of His rule but the heart of His presence. Here, God's divine plans for the universe—and for you—are being carried out. Think about that. God isn't distant or detached. His desire is to dwell with you, and His ultimate plan is to bring you into His presence, where there will be no more pain, no more separation—just eternal joy and peace.

Jesus gives us a powerful promise in John 14:2: "In my Father's house are many rooms... I go to prepare a place for you." This is personal.

God's ultimate desire is not only to rule but to welcome you into His home, His family, forever. He is not only a king but a loving father, preparing a place for His children.

The third heaven is also where His divine council gathers—a place filled with angelic beings who worship and serve Him day and night. Revelation 4:8 describes this scene: "Holy, holy, holy is the Lord God Almighty." Can you imagine such a place? A realm where worship never ceases and the glory of God fills every corner. This is the reality that He invites you to share.

As you reflect on the third heaven, understand that we are not just exploring a distant realm—we are exploring the very heart of God. The first heaven speaks of His provision, the second of His sovereignty and the spiritual battle that surrounds us, but the third heaven reveals His deepest desire: to be with us.

Conclusion: Part of a Divine Story

So, the next time you look up at the sky, remember: you are part of a grand, divine story. Each heaven—the sky above, the starry expanse, and the very throne room of God—reflects a deeper truth about who God is and what He desires for you. The first heaven reminds us of His provision, the second heaven points to His sovereignty and the reality of spiritual warfare, and the third heaven reveals His ultimate goal: to dwell with His people forever.

God reigns supreme over the heavens and the earth, and no matter what happens—whether in this world or in the spiritual realm—His purpose will prevail. His heart is for you, and His ultimate desire is to bring you into His presence forever. That's the truth of Scripture, and it's the truth for you.

Jeremiah 10:12

It is he who made the earth by his power,
who established the world by his wisdom,
and by his understanding stretched out the heavens

.

Chapter 4 - Unveiling the Spiritual Realm
A Journey Beyond the Visible

As we stand in awe of the third heaven—the place where God's glory dwells—we now turn our attention to the spiritual beings who inhabit this vast, unseen realm. Just as the heavens declare God's majesty, so too do the creatures who serve Him, each reflecting His power, wisdom, and justice in their unique roles. But before we proceed, take a deep breath. Are you ready to step into something truly awe-inspiring?

Have you ever wondered what lies beyond the world we can see?

It's easy to get absorbed in the rhythm of daily life—our relationships, challenges, and routines. Yet, as we've begun to explore, there's a far greater reality. An unseen world pulses with divine life and purpose, a realm that existed long before the earth or humanity. Today, we'll peel back the veil to glimpse this magnificent domain, where divine beings, created with purpose and beauty, reflect God's glory.

Just as God spoke the universe into existence with love and power, He established a spiritual realm inhabited by a heavenly family—beings who commune with Him and carry out His will. Who are these celestial beings? What roles do they play in God's overarching plan for creation? These questions invite us to step deeper into the mystery of the unseen realm.

The Heavenly Host: God's Spiritual Family

When many hear the term Elohim, they think of it as another name for Yahweh, the God of Israel. While this is true in some contexts, Elohim actually refers to all spiritual beings in the heavenly realm. The Bible uses Elohim not only for Yahweh but also for other divine entities—

sometimes called "gods" (with a lowercase g). Yet Yahweh is the one true Elohim who reigns supreme over all creation.

To clarify, Elohim can be tricky because, while it often refers to Yahweh, the one true God, it can also be used more broadly to describe any spiritual being in the heavenly realm. These "gods" are not rivals to Yahweh but rather created beings who exist within His divine order. Yahweh alone is the Supreme Elohim, ruling over all other spiritual beings, as we see in Psalm 82:1, where God takes His place in the divine council to judge among these "gods."

For example, Psalm 82:1 says, "God [Elohim] has taken His place in the divine council; in the midst of the gods [elohim], He holds judgment." Here, Elohim refers both to Yahweh and other divine beings in His heavenly council. While many spiritual beings exist, they are all subject to Yahweh's authority.

This hierarchy is further illustrated in Deuteronomy 32:8, where the "sons of God" (bene Elohim) are given governance over nations. These spiritual beings, though powerful, operate within God's sovereign plan. Job 1:6 offers another glimpse into this divine council, where the "sons of God" present themselves before the Lord, including Satan, a rebellious member of this celestial family.

Understanding the broader use of Elohim reveals a rich, multi-layered spiritual world where divine beings interact with God and humanity. Though Yahweh reigns supreme, He invites these beings to participate in His cosmic governance, reflecting His relational nature. Just as He desires communion with humanity, He also engages with His heavenly family.

Seraphim and Cherubim: Guardians of God's Throne

Among Yahweh's spiritual servants, two classes of beings stand out for their proximity to His divine presence—the Seraphim and Cherubim.

These radiant, awe-inspiring creatures reveal essential truths about God's character and His relationship with creation.

The Seraphim: Ministers of Holiness

In Isaiah 6:1-7, the Seraphim are depicted as six-winged beings who dwell in the immediate presence of God. With two wings, they cover their faces in reverence, with two they cover their feet in humility, and with two they fly. These beings cry out, "Holy, holy, holy is the Lord of hosts; the whole earth is full of His glory!" Their chorus shakes the very foundations of heaven, drawing all creation into worship.

The Seraphim's fiery brilliance reflects God's holiness, and their actions speak of transformation. One Seraph touches a burning coal to Isaiah's lips, purifying him for divine service. This moment reveals that the Seraphim are not just worshipers but also agents of God's cleansing power. Through them, we are reminded of God's desire to purify and transform us, making us fit to reflect His glory.

The Cherubim: Protectors of Divine Order

But while the Seraphim reveal God's holiness, another group of spiritual beings reflects His role as protector and guardian of divine order—the Cherubim.

First mentioned in Genesis 3:24, the Cherubim guard the way to Eden with flaming swords after humanity's fall, a symbol of God's justice and the separation sin creates. These mighty beings are also depicted atop the Ark of the Covenant, their wings outstretched over the mercy seat, where God's presence would meet His people. In this role, the Cherubim represent God's grace and protection. They are not merely guards; they are active participants in maintaining divine order.

Together, the Seraphim and Cherubim remind us that God's realm is one of both awe-inspiring holiness and profound protection. Their roles reflect God's dual nature as both purifier and guardian, inviting us to reverence and trust.

The Ophanim: Wheels of Divine Justice

And yet, God's creation extends even further. Within His celestial administration are other awe-inspiring beings who symbolize His justice and authority—beings like the Ophanim.

Ezekiel's vision of the Ophanim—strange, awe-inspiring "wheels within wheels" covered with eyes—reveals another layer of God's celestial administration. Described in Ezekiel 1 and 10, these beings symbolize God's omniscience and omnipresence. The wheels' movement in every direction without turning mirrors the boundless scope of God's authority.

The Ophanim, often overlooked in biblical commentary, serve as a vivid reminder of God's constant vigilance. Their countless eyes see all, symbolizing God's intimate knowledge of creation. They represent divine justice in motion, ensuring that God's decrees are executed across both heaven and earth with perfect precision.

Powers, Authorities, and Dominions: Guardians of Divine Law

Beyond the immediate throne room of God, we encounter the Powers, Authorities, and Dominions—spiritual forces that govern the order of creation and carry out God's sovereign rule across the cosmos. Together, they form a hierarchy of celestial beings responsible for maintaining balance and order throughout the spiritual and physical realms.

Powers and Dominions: Enforcers of Divine Will

In Ephesians 6:12, the Apostle Paul refers to these beings when he describes the spiritual forces we wrestle against: "the rulers, the authorities, and the cosmic powers over this present darkness." Powers and Dominions, in particular, oversee the cosmic order, acting as enforcers of divine justice and ensuring that God's will is executed throughout creation.

When aligned with God's purpose, these beings inspire and guide national leaders toward justice, mercy, and godly governance. They play a key role in ensuring that societies reflect divine principles. However, when corrupted or aligned with rebellious forces, Powers and Dominions can contribute to moral decay, influencing societies to turn away from God's design.

Authorities: Executors of Divine Judgment

Authorities, also referred to as Virtues in some traditions, have the role of executing God's judgments and maintaining order in both the heavenly and earthly realms. They act as intermediaries between heaven and earth, ensuring that God's will is carried out with precision and swiftness. When nations or rulers act out of alignment with God's justice, Authorities are responsible for intervening, either to restore order or to execute divine decrees.

These spiritual beings are crucial to maintaining the delicate balance of God's creation, ensuring that the world operates according to divine principles. Whether guiding nations toward righteousness or executing judgment, Powers, Dominions, and Authorities collectively work to uphold the overarching order established by God.

Archangels, Principalities, and Angels: Warriors and Guardians

Turning to the next tier of spiritual beings, we encounter Archangels, Principalities, and Angels, who are charged with more direct interaction with humanity and the physical world. These beings engage in both spiritual warfare and governance, influencing the fate of nations and individuals alike.

Archangels: Leaders of Heaven's Armies

Archangels stand at the forefront of God's celestial army, commanding vast legions of angels in spiritual warfare and protecting God's people from the forces of darkness. Two Archangels are particularly prominent in scripture—Michael and Gabriel.

Michael, as depicted in Revelation 12:7-9, leads the heavenly forces in battle against Satan and his fallen angels, casting them out of heaven. His role as the protector of Israel (Daniel 10:21) and God's people places him at the forefront of spiritual warfare, defending against demonic forces that seek to corrupt God's creation.

Gabriel, on the other hand, is best known for his role as God's messenger, delivering divine revelations to humanity. He reveals visions of the future to Daniel (Daniel 8, 9) and announces the birth of Christ to Mary (Luke 1), acting as a bridge between the divine and the earthly. Gabriel's role is less about warfare and more about guiding humanity through key moments of divine revelation.

Principalities: Guardians of Nations

Principalities serve as spiritual governors, overseeing nations and regions and ensuring that God's purposes for humanity are carried out on a national scale. They act as protectors and guides, often influencing the rise and fall of nations. Their role in the heavenly hierarchy reflects the importance God places on order and governance within His creation.

However, not all Principalities remain loyal to God. In Daniel 10:13, the "Prince of Persia," a fallen Principality, opposes God's messenger, delaying a critical revelation to Daniel. This celestial battle reveals the influence Principalities can have on the course of human events. Some, like the Prince of Persia, rebel against God's will, while others, like Michael, intervene to ensure that God's plan prevails.

Holy Principalities work to guide nations toward righteousness, influencing leaders to pursue justice and godly wisdom. But fallen Principalities, aligned with malevolent forces, lead nations into chaos, corruption, and idolatry. Understanding their role highlights the spiritual battle underlying world events and reminds us that the fate of nations is not purely a human affair but part of a larger cosmic struggle.

Angels: Messengers and Protectors

Angels, though often viewed as messengers, also serve as warriors and protectors in the ongoing spiritual warfare. Throughout scripture, they act as God's emissaries, delivering divine messages and guarding the faithful from harm. In 2 Kings 6:16-17, for example, Elisha's servant's eyes are opened to see the angelic host protecting them from enemy armies, a vivid reminder of the unseen forces at work in our lives.

These spiritual battles are not distant, abstract events—they have real implications for your life. Just as Daniel experienced delay due to the forces opposing him, we, too, face unseen obstacles in our own journeys. Yet, just as God sent His angels to fight for Daniel, He is also at work in your life, sending His heavenly hosts to guide, protect, and defend you in ways you may never fully see.

Angels not only deliver God's word but also engage in battle alongside Archangels and Principalities. Revelation 12:7 describes Angels fighting alongside Michael to cast Satan from heaven, underscoring their role as both messengers and warriors in God's cosmic plan.

A Glimpse into the Divine Plan

The spiritual realm is vast and filled with beings that reflect God's majesty, justice, and holiness. From the Seraphim and Cherubim who dwell in God's immediate presence, to the Powers, Dominions, and Authorities who influence the order of creation, to the Archangels, Principalities, and Angels who fight and protect on our behalf—each plays a role in God's divine order.

As we reflect on these beings and their roles, we are reminded that we, too, are part of a cosmic story. Our daily lives may seem mundane, but they are interwoven with this spiritual reality. The forces of light and darkness, of holiness and rebellion, shape the world in ways both seen and unseen.

And yet, above all these beings, Yahweh reigns supreme. His love, justice, and purpose extend across all realms, and He invites us to participate in His divine plan. Let this journey into the spiritual realm deepen our reverence for God and inspire us to live in harmony with His will, knowing we are always watched over, always loved.

Psalm 103:20

Bless the Lord, O you his angels, you mighty ones who do his word, obeying the voice of his word

Chapter 5 - In His Image:
Earth, Humanity, and the Grand Design

So far, we've journeyed through the creation of the heavens, reflected on the spiritual realms, explored the roles of divine beings, and witnessed the mysteries surrounding Lucifer's fall. Now, as we shift our focus to the physical world, we enter a pivotal moment in God's grand narrative—a moment where everything converges. Here, the divine and human stories begin to intertwine in the most extraordinary way.

In the previous chapters, we caught glimpses of the spiritual hierarchy and God's divine council, but now things become more intimate. God's creative power turns toward something new—something not just grand, but deeply personal. In this chapter, we step into the story where the spiritual and physical worlds collide. This isn't just about the creation of Earth; it's about God's desire for connection, for relationship, for partnership with His creation. Earth becomes the stage, not only for the unfolding of human history but for the continuation of a spiritual battle that began long before humanity even existed.

The Genesis of Earth: A Divine Masterpiece

Let's begin at the very start. The Bible opens with a proclamation that rings with authority and purpose: "In the beginning, God created the heavens and the earth" (Genesis 1:1). We've already explored the creation of the heavens, but now God's creative hand moves toward the physical. This single verse beautifully ties the spiritual and physical realms together. Just as the heavens were carefully crafted, so too was the Earth, which would soon become the home of God's physical family—us.

At first, the Earth was formless—a blank canvas hovering in the void, waiting for God's touch. And then, with the powerful words, "Let there be light," everything changes (Genesis 1:3). Imagine that moment: chaos turning to order, darkness giving way to light. What must it have been like to witness the first burst of radiance, the very beginning of life and structure? God's command brings forth creation from nothing. The physical world, like the heavens before it, is born from His deliberate and creative will. Day by day, He shapes the Earth with precision, separating light from darkness, land from sea, and filling it with life—all reflecting His divine order. Just as the heavens were structured with purpose, so too does the Earth mirror that intentional design.

The Pre-Flood World: A Forgotten Age

Before we continue with the creation of humanity, have you ever wondered what the Earth was like before the Flood? Genesis gives us a glimpse of this forgotten world. Initially, the Earth was covered by primal waters, a balance of forces waiting for God's hand to shape them. When He separated the waters to create the sky and the seas (Genesis 1:6-7), He wasn't just making space for life; He was creating an environment uniquely designed to thrive.

Above the Earth, a protective canopy of waters formed—a perfect environment where life flourished and where humans lived for centuries. The longevity of early humanity, their extended lifespans far beyond what we can imagine today, was a reflection of this pristine creation. It was a world of balance and abundance. Yet, as we will later see in the days of Noah, this ideal world was radically altered. The waters above and below were unleashed in a flood that would reshape the entire planet.

But for now, let us pause and recognize the beauty of this world before its fall—a world meticulously ordered by God, where every element, from the skies above to the seas below, served a deliberate purpose.

The Creation of Humanity: Imagers of God

Now, we arrive at the pinnacle of creation: humanity. On the sixth day, God declares, "Let us make man in our image, after our likeness" (Genesis 1:26). Pause for a moment and consider the profound weight of that statement. God's words reveal something intimate, something uniquely personal about His plan for humanity. When God says "us," we see the beauty of the Trinity at work, a communion of Father, Son, and Holy Spirit. Some scholars also suggest this moment may have been witnessed by the Divine Council—spiritual beings observing the creation of a new kind of being, one who would reflect God's nature in ways nothing else in creation could.

In Job 38:4-7, God asks, "Where were you when I laid the foundation of the earth?... when the morning stars sang together, and all the sons of God shouted for joy?" The heavens watched in awe as God formed humanity, the crown of creation. But what does it mean to be made in God's image? We are not like the rest of creation. We are designed to reflect God's qualities—love, reason, creativity, and so much more.

And God didn't just speak us into existence as He did with the rest of creation. This was personal. He formed us from the dust of the Earth, shaping us with His own hands, and then breathed His very breath into our lungs (Genesis 2:7). Can you feel the closeness in that act? It wasn't merely creation—it was a moment of divine intimacy.

The Grand Design: Order, Purpose, and Goodness

When God finished His work, He looked at all He had made and declared it "very good" (Genesis 1:31). This was more than an observation of beauty—it was a declaration of harmony, both moral and relational. Humanity, created in the image of God, wasn't a passive part of creation. We were given a role. Just as the Divine Council oversees the spiritual realm, we were called to oversee the physical one. We were entrusted with the care of the Earth, reflecting God's authority, creativity, and love in our stewardship.

At the heart of this creation mandate is the Imago Dei—the image of God. It is this identity that sets us apart from all other creatures. Our ability to reason, to love, to create, and to engage in meaningful relationships are all reflections of the Creator. And just as the members of the Divine Council were given authority in the spiritual realm, we've been given authority on Earth. But this authority is not about power; it's about responsibility.

The Imago Dei: Reflections of the Creator

Being made in God's image means that every person, regardless of status or ability, holds inherent worth and dignity. We are called to rule over creation with love and justice, embodying the attributes of the God who made us. As you reflect on this, consider: How do you see the Imago Dei in your daily life? How can you reflect God's character in the way you care for the world and the people around you?

Our role as stewards of creation is not just a privilege—it is a sacred trust. We are invited to participate in the flourishing of all life, reflecting God's goodness in every corner of the world. How do you engage with this call? How do you contribute to the care of God's creation, in both big and small ways?

Eden's Paradise: Where Heaven Met Earth

Now, we find ourselves at the threshold of Eden—a place where heaven and earth once intertwined in perfect harmony. Eden wasn't just a physical home for Adam and Eve; it was a cosmic temple, a divine meeting place where God, His spiritual family, and humanity could dwell together in intimate communion. Imagine this space: a lush garden teeming with life, the fragrance of blossoms in the air, and the sound of gentle streams flowing nearby. This wasn't just any garden—it was a realm of divine harmony, where God's presence was palpable, and the connection between His spiritual and physical families was beautifully alive.

Yet, even in this paradise, a moment of cosmic tension was brewing. The harmony was fragile, and a choice was looming—one that would shatter the peace of Eden and reverberate throughout history. What must it have felt like to walk in Eden before that choice was made? To experience perfect peace, only to feel it slipping away?

The story of creation is not just a distant past—it is the origin of the tension we live with today. We are the inheritors of a choice made in Eden, one that echoes through time. As we step into the next chapter, we will explore the mysteries of Eden and uncover its role as the ultimate intersection between the spiritual and physical realms. We will witness how a single decision in paradise reshaped the course of human history and points us toward the hope of restoration through Christ. Are you ready to continue this remarkable journey with me?

Genesis 1:2

The earth was without form and void, and darkness was over the face of the deep. And the Spirit of God was hovering over the face of the waters.

Origins of Disobedience

Genesis 2:9-10

And out of the ground the Lord God made to spring up every tree that is pleasant to the sight and good for food. The tree of life was in the midst of the garden, and the tree of the knowledge of good and evil. A river flowed out of Eden to water the garden, and there it divided and became four rivers.

Chapter 6 – Eden:
The Convergence of Heaven and Earth

Imagine the Garden of Eden not merely as a place of beauty and abundance, but as the first earthly temple of God—a sacred sanctuary where heaven and earth converged. More than just a garden, Eden was the heartbeat of creation, a divine meeting place where the seen and unseen were intricately woven together by the hand of God. In this holy space, humanity experienced unbroken communion with the Creator, worshiping not in temples made by human hands, but in a living, breathing sanctuary designed by God Himself.

The Bible tells us, "The Lord God planted a garden in Eden, in the east, and there He put the man whom He had formed" (Genesis 2:8). This was no ordinary garden; it was the dwelling place of God with His creation, the meeting point of heaven and earth. Here, God's presence was not hidden but tangible—felt in the breeze, seen in the shimmering leaves, and heard in the song of the rivers that watered the earth (Genesis 2:10). Eden was the sacred space where humanity and the divine were united, a place where Adam walked with God "in the cool of the day" (Genesis 3:8).

A Seamless Transition: From Humanity's Creation to Their Divine Purpose

In the previous chapter, we explored how humanity was created in God's image (Genesis 1:27), yet the full realization of this divine calling came when Adam was placed in Eden, the sacred space where God's presence dwelt. In this garden, Adam's role as God's image-bearer was fully expressed through his priestly vocation. As Scripture says, "The Lord God took the man and put him in the garden of Eden to work it and keep it" (Genesis 2:15). The Hebrew terms for "work" (abad) and "keep" (shamar) are the same terms later used to describe the duties of priests in the Tabernacle (Numbers 3:7-8). Eden was more than a garden—it was a temple, and Adam was its priest, called to worship, tend, and protect this holy space.

Eve, created as a partner for Adam (Genesis 2:18-23), shared in this divine stewardship. Together, they were the co-stewards of creation, reflecting the fullness of humanity's divine purpose. Their calling was not one of toil or mere caretaking but a priestly partnership in the worship of God and the flourishing of His creation.

Eden: The First Temple of God's Presence

Eden was the first temple on earth, the original Holy of Holies. Genesis 2:9 describes how God caused to grow "every tree that is pleasant to the sight and good for food," a reflection of the abundance of God's presence. The rivers flowing from Eden (Genesis 2:10-14) symbolized the life-giving presence of God, much like the rivers of living water seen in Ezekiel's vision of the temple (Ezekiel 47) and in John's vision of the New Jerusalem (Revelation 22). These rivers were not just geographical features but represented the spiritual reality that God's presence flowed out from Eden to all creation.

The structure of Eden prefigured the later temples of Israel, particularly the Holy of Holies where God's glory would dwell. Just as the High Priest would enter the Holy of Holies to meet with God (Leviticus 16:2), Adam enjoyed unmediated access to the divine, walking with God in perfect communion. In Eden, the presence of God was not veiled by curtains or separated by rituals—it was experienced directly.

Adam: The First Priest of God's Sacred Space

Adam's priestly role in Eden is further emphasized by the command to "work" and "keep" the garden (Genesis 2:15). These are the same words used to describe the responsibilities of the Levites in the Tabernacle, highlighting the sacred nature of Adam's task. As the first priest, Adam's role extended beyond tending the garden's physical aspects; he was responsible for guarding the holiness of the space.

As a priest, Adam was called to protect Eden from any desecration, a role foreshadowing the entrance of the serpent (Genesis 3:1). His duty to guard the sanctity of God's first temple mirrors the role of the priests and Levites who guarded the later earthly temples from defilement (Numbers 3:38). The garden was not merely a place for agriculture; it was a holy space that Adam was entrusted to defend.

Eden as a Cosmic Temple: A Gathering of Heaven and Earth

Eden was not just the first temple—it was a cosmic meeting place where heaven and earth intersected. Scripture often associates temples with mountains, and Ezekiel 28:13-14 refers to Eden as "the holy mountain of God." This suggests that Eden was a high place, spiritually elevated, symbolizing its connection to heaven. The imagery of a mountain temple signifies a place where the divine council gathered, and where heaven touched earth.

Adam, as the priest of this cosmic temple, mirrored the work of the divine council. Just as spiritual beings participated in God's governance of the heavens (Psalm 82), Adam was entrusted with governing the earth. His priestly service in Eden was not merely personal—it was cosmic, a reflection of God's relational nature, inviting both heavenly and earthly beings to participate in His governance.

The rivers flowing from Eden, like those in Ezekiel's vision and in Revelation, carried God's life-giving presence to the farthest reaches of creation. Eden was the original Holy of Holies, the source from which God's presence spread into the world.

Eden: The Blueprint for All Temples

Eden was the archetype for all future temples. The Tabernacle, the Temple of Solomon, and even the New Jerusalem in Revelation all reflect the structure and purpose of Eden. Just as Eden was a place where God dwelled with humanity, the Tabernacle and Temple served the same purpose (Exodus 25:8). They were sacred spaces where priests served, sacrifices were made, and God's glory was manifest.

Adam's priesthood in Eden prefigured the Levitical priesthood. His call to "work" and "keep" the garden echoed the work of the priests in the later temples. Eden, however, also points to a future reality: the time when heaven and earth will once again be united, when God's presence will dwell fully with humanity, and creation will be restored to its original purpose (Revelation 21:3-4).

The Hope of Restoration

Eden gives us a glimpse of the perfection of God's creation, where heaven and earth, humanity and the divine, existed in complete harmony. It was a sanctuary where every living being, tree, and river reflected the Creator's glory. But as we will see in the next section, this perfection was fragile. The serpent's entrance into Eden (Genesis 3:1) set in motion a disruption that would shatter this peace, desecrating the first temple.

Yet even in the midst of this coming rebellion, there is hope. God's plan for restoration was already taking shape. Through Jesus Christ, the ultimate High Priest, what was lost in Eden will be restored. The temple of God's presence will once again be among us, and His glory will fill the earth as it did in the beginning (Revelation 21:22-23).

Introduction to Section 2 / "Rebellion"

From the earliest moments of creation, the universe has been a place of profound beauty and order, but also of tension. As long as there has been light, darkness has sought to encroach upon it. Rebellion, both celestial and human, is a theme woven through the fabric of creation. But why? Why do beings, whether angelic or human, turn against the divine order? These questions have captivated hearts and minds for millennia, inviting us to reflect on the nature of free will, disobedience, and the far-reaching consequences of rebellion. This section is an invitation—not just to witness rebellion from a distance, but to wrestle with its meaning and its relevance in our own lives. Together, we step into a story that spans the heavens and the earth—a cosmic drama of pride, defiance, and, ultimately, redemption.

We begin by turning our gaze toward a figure whose name once meant "light bearer": Lucifer. Created with brilliance and beauty, Lucifer held a place of honor in God's divine council. But his story is a cautionary tale, revealing how even the brightest of beings can fall victim to pride. How could one so close to God's throne seek it for himself? What does Lucifer's rebellion teach us about the nature of power, ambition, and the fine line between worship and self-exaltation?

Imagine standing at the edge of heaven, watching as the bright morning star begins to dim. This is the moment where divine order cracks and rebellion first takes root. Lucifer's radiant beginning and tragic fall serve as a warning—pride has the power to corrupt even the most exalted beings. His defiance marks the start of a cosmic conflict that will ripple through both the spiritual and physical realms.

From this celestial drama, we move to the next great turning point: the fall of Satan from heaven. His rebellion, once confined to the spiritual realm, now spills into the earth. Banished from heaven, Satan's influence begins to take root in human history, as the struggle between good and evil shifts from the heavenly courts to the earth itself. Here, we uncover the deeper dynamics of spiritual warfare—how rebellion in the heavens intersects with the choices made on earth.

But the story does not end there. In the Garden of Eden, Satan assumes a new role—the serpent, a figure cloaked in deception and cunning. It is here that humanity's own struggle with rebellion begins. In the lush garden, where heaven and earth once converged, Satan lures Adam and Eve into a fateful choice that shatters the harmony of creation. In this chapter, we will explore the nature of temptation—how evil often masquerades as something desirable—and how humanity's disobedience sets in motion a ripple effect that reverberates through time.

With Adam and Eve's choice, the door to sin and suffering swings wide open. What follows is the moral unraveling of humanity. From the first murder to widespread corruption, the world descends into chaos. And yet, even in this darkness, there are glimpses of God's enduring hope for redemption. As we trace the ripple effects of rebellion from the Garden to the days of Noah, we witness how disobedience spreads like a contagion, growing from individual choices to infect entire communities and civilizations. This is a reminder that rebellion, once introduced, is not easily contained.

But rebellion is not confined to the earth. Our journey will take us back to the heavens, where divine beings—known as the sons of God—engage in their own act of defiance. They abandon their divine responsibilities and pursue earthly pleasures, resulting in the birth of the Nephilim—mysterious giants whose presence on earth disrupts the natural order. Through their story, we will reflect on the boundaries between the divine and the human, and how crossing those boundaries leads to devastating consequences for all of creation.

As the world spirals deeper into wickedness, God's response is both swift and severe: the Flood, an act of divine judgment and mercy. The waters cleanse the earth, wiping away the corruption that has overtaken creation. Yet, within this judgment, there is mercy. God preserves a remnant—Noah and his family—through whom His promise endures. This chapter invites us to reflect on the balance between justice and grace, and the enduring hope of renewal, even in the face of destruction.

However, even after the cleansing waters of the Flood, rebellion reemerges. Humanity, though given a fresh start, quickly reverts to old patterns of pride and disobedience. This brings us to the Tower of Babel, where humanity once again seeks to "reach the heavens," challenging God's authority with collective ambition. Through this story, we see how rebellion is not just about individual disobedience, but about humanity's desire for independence from the Creator. Babel's fall marks a critical turning point in the narrative, scattering humanity and disinheriting the nations, placing them under the influence of rebellious spiritual rulers.

As we explore the disinheritance of nations, we will witness the rise of idolatry and spiritual corruption, as fallen beings—false gods—lead the nations astray. The division of the world into lands ruled by rebellious powers raises profound questions about authority, allegiance, and the ongoing battle between light and darkness.

Together, these narratives weave a tapestry of rebellion—one that spans both heaven and earth, involving divine and human beings, each grappling with the gift and burden of free will. These stories challenge us to consider the nature of rebellion, not just as something that belongs to ancient times, but as a force that is still at work in our world today. How do we respond to the temptations and deceptions that seek to pull us away from God's design? Where do we see the echoes of Lucifer's pride, Adam's disobedience, and Babel's ambition in our own lives?

As we embark on this exploration of rebellion, we do so with the understanding that this is not the end of the story. Even in the midst of defiance, God's plan for redemption is already at work. The fall is not final. Each act of rebellion reveals the need for restoration, and through Christ, the hope of renewal is promised.

Let us now step into the heart of this cosmic struggle—into a world where rebellion has fractured the divine order, but where the seeds of redemption are already beginning to grow. For in understanding rebellion, we may better understand grace.

Chapter 7 - The Bright Star: Lucifer's Radiant Beginning

As we continue our journey into the nature of rebellion, we turn our gaze toward the first and most significant act of defiance in the spiritual realm—the rebellion of Lucifer. His fall from grace stands as the original fracture in the divine order, a rebellion that has rippled through both the heavens and the earth. Before his infamous revolt, however, Lucifer held a place of supreme honor and brilliance, standing at the pinnacle of God's creation. His story, marked by both breathtaking beauty and tragic pride, offers profound insights into the risks of free will and the consequences of rebellion. Today, we peel back the layers of this complex being to examine who Lucifer was before his fall and how his defiance set the stage for a cosmic conflict that continues to shape the narrative of redemption we've been exploring.

A Vision of Radiance

Imagine, for a moment, a being whose very essence illuminated the heavens with the brilliance of divine light—Lucifer, whose name means "light bearer." He was more than just another celestial being; he was created to reflect the glory and wisdom of God in a way that no other being could. Each facet of his being shimmered with divine radiance, and his form was adorned with precious stones, each one glistening with the splendor of the Creator's design. Lucifer wasn't just beautiful—he was the epitome of perfection.

Before we even consider his fall, we must first understand the incredible heights from which he came. In Ezekiel 28:12, we read that Lucifer was "the signet of perfection, full of wisdom and perfect in beauty." His brilliance wasn't merely aesthetic; it was a reflection of his divine role. Lucifer was entrusted with intimate proximity to God, serving as an anointed cherub—a guardian of the divine presence, standing near the throne of the Almighty. His presence in the heavenly court was a testament to God's craftsmanship and the harmonious order of the spiritual realm.

A Role of Honor in the Third Heaven

Lucifer's position in the spiritual hierarchy was one of profound significance. In the Third Heaven, where God's presence dwells in full majesty, Lucifer occupied an exalted status. He was not a mere spectator of God's glory—he was a minister of it. As an anointed cherub, Lucifer acted as a bridge between the divine and the created world, radiating the light of God's presence throughout the heavens. His brilliance wasn't just a symbol of his beauty—it was an instrument of God's purpose, reflecting the Creator's glory to all of creation.

As a member of God's Divine Council, Lucifer played a pivotal role in the governance of creation, offering his wisdom and insight during the deliberations of the heavenly host. This council represented the divine order, where every being had a unique role to sustain the universe's harmony. Within this hierarchy, Lucifer's position was one of prominence and authority, inspiring awe and reverence among the other celestial beings. He guided them in their worship and service to God, a task that further highlighted his significance.

But even in this exalted role, one profound truth remains: no being, no matter how radiant or honored, is immune to the dangers of free will.

Free Will: The Risk of Rebellion

Here, we return to a concept that we've explored before—free will, the ability to choose. Just as humanity was endowed with this gift, so too were the spiritual beings. God designed this freedom as a precious gift that would allow love and relationship to flourish. True love, after all, cannot be forced; it must be chosen. And so, it was with Lucifer. He had the freedom to remain in the light or to turn away from it.

Yet, free will is a double-edged sword. The same freedom that allowed Lucifer to bask in the glory of God also opened the door to rebellion. Tragically, he chose to misuse this freedom, turning away from the very purpose for which he was created. It is a sobering reminder that freedom, while beautiful, also carries the risk of rejection. In a moment of pride, Lucifer stepped through that door, making a choice that would not only alter his destiny but would impact the entire cosmos.

The Seeds of Rebellion

What drove Lucifer to make this fateful choice? Scripture offers glimpses into the pride that led to his downfall. In Isaiah 14:12, we read a haunting image: "How you are fallen from heaven, O Day Star, son of Dawn! How you are cut down to the ground..." Pride lay at the root of Lucifer's rebellion. His heart swelled with a desire for something beyond his created purpose. He declared, "I will make myself like the Most High" (Isaiah 14:14). He yearned not to serve God but to rival Him, seeking equality with the Almighty.

This ambition is strikingly familiar, isn't it? It mirrors the temptation that humanity would later face in the Garden of Eden—the desire to "be like God" and claim the knowledge of good and evil for oneself. Lucifer's rebellion set a tragic pattern that humanity would follow. Just as Lucifer sought to elevate himself beyond his appointed role, so too did Adam and Eve attempt to step out of their designed place, choosing self-exaltation over submission to their Creator.

The Cosmic Implications

Lucifer's rebellion was not merely a personal fall from grace; it was a cosmic event that disrupted the entire spiritual order. Just as Adam and Eve's disobedience would affect all of humanity, Lucifer's pride sent shockwaves through the heavens. This was not an isolated act of defiance. It introduced a rift between good and evil that reverberates throughout both the spiritual and physical realms to this day.

Free will, as we've seen, is a precious gift. But when misused, it becomes a force for destruction. In Lucifer's case, his fall didn't just impact him—it set the stage for a spiritual conflict that continues to shape the course of history. His rebellion was the catalyst for a battle between good and evil, a battle that continues to influence the world we live in today.

Looking Forward: The Fall of Lucifer

But Lucifer's rebellion did not go unanswered. God, in His sovereignty, would not allow such defiance to go unchallenged. What began as pride blossomed into full-scale revolt, and Lucifer was cast out of heaven. Yet, this is not where his story ends.

As we move forward, we will explore the aftermath of Lucifer's fall—his transformation into Satan, the adversary—and how his defiance triggered a cosmic struggle that continues to ripple through both the spiritual and physical realms. His rebellion was not just a moment of personal pride, but the beginning of a spiritual war that would shape the destiny of creation.

Conclusion: The Lessons of Lucifer's Fall

As we close this chapter and prepare to turn the page, let us hold onto the lessons we've uncovered. Lucifer's story is not simply about the fall of one radiant being; it's a reflection on the risks of freedom, the destructive power of pride, and the ongoing battle for the hearts of both spiritual beings and humanity. His choice to misuse his gift of free will set in motion a cosmic struggle, one that echoes throughout the heavens and earth.

In our next step together, we will trace the ripple effects of Lucifer's fall across creation, uncovering deeper truths about the nature of rebellion, the cosmic conflict between good and evil, and how God's redemptive plan is at work, even in the midst of darkness.

Chapter 8 – The Two Falls: Lucifer's Rebellion and Satan's Banishment

Imagine standing at the crossroads of heaven and earth, witnessing the moment where rebellion shattered the divine order. It's here, at this juncture, that we encounter one of the most pivotal moments in Scripture: Lucifer's fall. Until now, we've explored the eternal nature of God (Chapter 1), His deliberate design of creation (Chapter 2), and the majestic hierarchy of the heavenly realms, including the Divine Council (Chapter 3). But now, the narrative takes a darker turn as we confront the story of Lucifer, the "Bright Star," whose pride and ambition led to a rebellion that forever altered the course of both the spiritual and physical realms.

Lucifer's fall isn't just the story of one being's descent; it's a profound cosmic event that rippled through all of creation. In this chapter, we'll examine two critical stages of Lucifer's fall—his initial rebellion in heaven and his later, final banishment—and how these events continue to shape the ongoing battle between good and evil.

The First Fall: Lucifer's Rebellion in Heaven

To fully grasp the magnitude of Lucifer's rebellion, we must first revisit his original position among the heavenly host. In the previous chapters, we saw Lucifer's role as a radiant, wise, and exalted being, entrusted with immense authority in God's heavenly realm. He was created to reflect the brilliance and wisdom of his Creator, and his role was one of honor and responsibility.

Yet, with great power came a dangerous gift: free will. Like humanity, spiritual beings were given the freedom to choose—a gift meant to cultivate genuine love and worship. But this gift came with risk. In Lucifer's case, the risk turned into tragedy as pride took root in his heart. No longer content to reflect God's light, he desired to claim it for himself.

The prophet Ezekiel captures this tragic turn of events, saying, "Your heart was proud because of your beauty; you corrupted your wisdom for the sake of your splendor" (Ezekiel 28:17). Lucifer's beauty and brilliance, intended to glorify God, became the source of his downfall. He sought to elevate himself above his Creator, declaring, "I will make myself like the Most High" (Isaiah 14:14). Instead of ascending, however, he was cast down—"brought down to Sheol, to the far reaches of the pit" (Isaiah 14:15).

This first fall marked Lucifer's transformation into Satan, the adversary. Though he lost his position as the "Morning Star," he still retained a measure of access to the heavenly realms. As seen in the Book of Job, Satan could still present himself before God, accusing humanity: "Now there was a day when the sons of God came to present themselves before the Lord, and Satan also came among them" (Job 1:6). His role had shifted from that of a trusted servant to a bitter accuser, yet his access to heaven was not fully severed—at least, not yet.

The Second Fall: Satan's Banishment from Heaven

While Lucifer's first fall stripped him of his heavenly status, it was not his final expulsion. That would come later, after Christ's redemptive work on the cross. This is where we witness Satan's second fall, a permanent and complete banishment from heaven.

In Revelation 12, we are given a vivid account of a celestial battle, where Satan and his angels are finally cast out of heaven: "And the great dragon was thrown down, that ancient serpent, who is called the devil and Satan, the deceiver of the whole world—he was thrown down to the earth, and his angels were thrown down with him" (Revelation 12:9).

To fully understand the significance of this passage, it's important to consider the context. In Revelation 12, we see a great cosmic struggle that unfolds as a woman, often understood to represent Israel or the people of God, gives birth to a child, "a male child, one who is to rule all the nations" (Revelation 12:5). This child is widely interpreted as a reference to Christ, whose coming and victory over Satan would fulfill God's redemptive plan. After the child is caught up to God's throne (a clear reference to Christ's ascension), war breaks out in heaven. Michael and his angels fight against the dragon (Satan), and the result is Satan's final banishment from the heavenly realms.

This moment, described in Revelation, coincides with the victory of Christ through His death, resurrection, and ascension. It is Christ's triumph on the cross that decisively defeats Satan's ability to accuse humanity before God. We can be assured that this scripture refers to the time of Christ because it is immediately tied to His coming, His mission, and His triumph. Revelation 12:10-11 declares: "Now the salvation and the power and the kingdom of our God and the authority of his Christ have come, for the accuser of our brothers has been thrown down, who accuses them day and night before our God. And they have conquered him by the blood of the Lamb and by the word of their testimony, for they loved not their lives even unto death."

Satan's second fall was thus a direct result of Christ's victory. The "blood of the Lamb" broke the power of Satan's accusations, ensuring his defeat and revoking his access to the heavenly courts. Satan could no longer stand before God to accuse His people.

The Cosmic Consequences of Lucifer's Rebellion

The consequences of Lucifer's rebellion extend far beyond his own fall. His defiance disrupted the harmony of creation, introducing a spiritual conflict that now plays out across both the heavenly and earthly realms. His first fall signaled the beginning of a cosmic rebellion, and his second fall—his expulsion from heaven—shifted the battlefield to the earth.

Revelation 12:12 warns of this transition: "But woe to you, O earth and sea, for the devil has come down to you in great wrath, because he knows that his time is short!" Satan's fury, fueled by the knowledge that his ultimate defeat is imminent, is now directed toward humanity. While his final destruction is assured, Satan's influence continues to wreak havoc, sowing division, deception, and destruction in the world.

The Two Falls: Understanding the Distinction

To fully appreciate the significance of Satan's rebellion, we must distinguish between these two falls. Lucifer's first fall was the result of pride, ambition, and a desire to challenge God's authority. Though demoted from his position of honor, he still had access to God's court. The second fall, however, was a final and irrevocable expulsion—triggered by Christ's victory on the cross—which barred Satan from ever accusing God's people in the heavenly courts again.

Satan's final banishment from heaven in Revelation 12 marks a critical turning point in the cosmic conflict. As 1 John 3:8 reminds us, "The reason the Son of God appeared was to destroy the works of the devil." Christ's victory was not only about human salvation; it was a cosmic triumph over the forces of evil.

However, Satan's defeat in heaven does not mean the end of his influence. Revelation warns us that Satan, in his anger and desperation, now seeks to unleash his wrath on the earth, intensifying the spiritual battle that shapes human history.

From Many to One: The Evolution of Satan in Scripture

While Lucifer's rebellion is central to our understanding of spiritual warfare, it's important to note that the concept of "satan" in Scripture is broader than just one being. In the Old Testament, the term "satan" is often used to describe adversaries, both human and spiritual, who stand in opposition to God's will. This plural usage reminds us that the forces of rebellion are manifold, involving many different entities and influences.

Throughout Scripture, we encounter various "satans"—figures who oppose God's people and attempt to thwart His plans. Whether in the form of Pharaoh, King Saul, or other spiritual adversaries, the role of "satan" represents opposition to God's kingdom. However, over time, especially with the influence of early Christian thought, the figure of Satan became more personalized, coming to represent the singular embodiment of evil—the leader of all spiritual rebellion against God.

This evolution in understanding helps us grasp the broader spiritual dynamics at play in the Bible. The cosmic struggle is not limited to one being; it involves many forces of opposition, all seeking to defy God's order and disrupt His redemptive plan.

Looking Ahead: Creation, Humanity, and the Serpent's Role

As we conclude this chapter on Lucifer's two falls, we find ourselves standing at the threshold of another pivotal moment in the cosmic narrative—the creation of humanity and the entrance of the serpent into the story. The rebellion we've seen in the heavenly realms now takes shape on earth, as Satan—in the guise of the serpent—enters the Garden of Eden and tempts Adam and Eve, setting off a chain reaction of sin and disobedience that will reverberate throughout history.

In the next chapter, we will peel back the layers of deception surrounding the serpent in Eden, exploring how Satan's cunning led to humanity's fall and how this ancient foe continues to influence the world today. Just as Lucifer's rebellion disrupted the divine order in heaven, the serpent's deception in Eden shattered the harmony of God's creation on earth.

Genesis 3:2

Now the serpent was more crafty than any other beast of the field that the Lord God had made. He said to the woman, "Did God actually say, 'You shall not eat of any tree in the garden'?

Chapter 9 - The Ancient Foe: Unmasking the Serpent

Let's take a moment to reflect on our journey so far. Over the past chapters, we've explored the awe-inspiring beauty of God's creation and the heartbreaking tragedy of Lucifer's fall. Together, we've witnessed the intricate divine order woven into the very fabric of existence—a masterpiece of unimaginable beauty. Yet, that masterpiece was scarred by rebellion. As we move forward, we are about to confront even more troubling, yet essential, themes: spiritual rebellion and humanity's own disobedience.

In this next phase, we turn our attention to one of the most mysterious figures in Scripture—the serpent in the Garden of Eden. This serpent is far more than a mere creature; it represents an ancient and powerful force—a force whose influence reaches back into the heavens and continues to ripple through the world today. Together, we'll unravel how the serpent not only triggered humanity's fall but also marked a critical turning point in an ongoing cosmic struggle—a struggle that still affects our lives in ways both seen and unseen.

Illuminated Deceit: The Shining Serpent

When we first encounter the serpent in Genesis 3, it's tempting to see it as nothing more than a snake. But beneath the surface of the text, there is a deeper meaning. The Hebrew word for serpent, nachash (נָחָשׁ), can also be translated as "shining one" or "enchanter." This suggests that the serpent wasn't simply an ordinary animal but a spiritual being of extraordinary allure. This brings us back to something we've seen before in Lucifer's story—a being created to reflect the light of God, yet corrupted by pride and ambition.

Think back to Chapter 4, where we explored Lucifer's role before his fall. He was once the bright morning star, a radiant being who stood near God's throne. Now, compare that with the image of the serpent in Genesis 3. Both are described with similar language—beings who were once close to divine glory but became agents of deception. It's chilling, isn't it? The serpent is more than just an embodiment of temptation; it represents the same spirit of rebellion that led to Lucifer's fall. This connection shows that the serpent's deception wasn't just about tricking Adam and Eve—it was part of a larger cosmic rebellion aimed at subverting God's authority.

This insight into the serpent's true nature invites us to reflect on the deceptive forces at work in our own lives. Like Eve, we often encounter things that seem beautiful or wise, but beneath the surface, they are corrupt. Just as the serpent lured Eve with promises of enlightenment and power, so too does deception work its way into our lives, often cloaked in half-truths and alluring promises.

Unmasking the Serpent: A Deeper Look at the Fall

As we dive deeper into the Genesis 3 narrative, we start to unmask the serpent and its role in the larger story of cosmic rebellion. This is more than a simple tale of a snake tempting Eve; it is the opening act of a cosmic struggle that will span the entire Bible. In Ezekiel 28:13, we see a glimpse of a figure in Eden, adorned with beauty and precious stones, but who falls from glory. Many scholars believe this figure refers to Lucifer—or the serpent itself—revealing that the fall in Eden wasn't just a human event, but part of a broader spiritual rebellion.

The serpent's deception in Genesis 3 is cunning. It doesn't directly oppose God but twists His words. "You will not surely die," the serpent tells Eve, manipulating the truth and planting doubt about God's intentions (Genesis 3:4-5). The serpent's lie subtly suggests that God is holding something back, that true wisdom and autonomy lie outside His command. This mirrors Lucifer's own fall, where pride and the desire to "be like the Most High" led him astray (Isaiah 14:14).

The deception in the Garden of Eden wasn't just about that moment—it was a continuation of a rebellion that began long before, in the heavens. The serpent represents not only the temptation of humanity but also a deeper conflict between order and chaos, light and darkness. The nachash, the shining one, was more than a trickster—it was an agent of disruption, determined to undermine God's plan for creation.

This connection between the serpent and Lucifer becomes even clearer in Revelation 12:9, where the serpent is explicitly identified as Satan—"that ancient serpent, called the devil, who leads the whole world astray." This gives us a fuller picture of the serpent's role in the cosmic drama. The serpent is not just an enemy from the distant past—it is the embodiment of a force that has been waging war against God's creation since the dawn of time, a force that continues to work in the world today.

A Cosmic Battle—and a Promise of Redemption

To fully grasp the significance of the serpent in Eden, we must understand how this event fits into the larger biblical narrative of rebellion and redemption. The serpent's deception didn't just cause the fall of humanity—it set in motion the long arc of salvation history, a battle between good and evil that began in the garden and finds its climax in Christ.

But here's the crucial point: while the serpent-initiated humanity's downfall, God immediately set in motion a plan for redemption. In Genesis 3:15, we encounter the first glimpse of this redemptive plan, often referred to as the protoevangelium or the "first gospel". God promises that the offspring of the woman will one day crush the serpent's head. This points forward to Christ, the one who would ultimately defeat Satan and reverse the curse brought on by humanity's fall. While the serpent may have succeeded in introducing sin into the world, the story does not end in defeat. Through Christ, victory is assured, and the path back to the light of Eden is opened once again.

As we continue our journey together, let's keep this broader context in mind. The serpent's deception was powerful, but it was not the final word. The cosmic battle between good and evil continues, but we already know how it ends. Christ has won the victory, and through Him, we too can resist the serpent's lies and walk in the truth of God's light.

Let us move forward with eyes wide open to the struggles we face, but also with hearts filled with hope—hope that the serpent's defeat is already secured, and that God's redemptive plan will shine brighter than any darkness.

Transition to Next Chapter: The Serpent's Legacy

As we leave the Garden of Eden, the serpent's influence doesn't fade; in fact, it expands. The deception that began in the garden set a pattern of rebellion that echoes throughout human history. In the next chapter, we will dive deeper into how this ancient foe—Satan—has continued to twist, deceive, and wage war against humanity. From his role as the tempter to his efforts to corrupt the nations, we will unmask the ongoing tactics of the enemy, who remains relentless in his quest to lead the world astray.

But, just as before, we won't journey through these dark truths without the light of God's promise leading the way. The serpent may have struck, but through Christ, the ultimate redeemer, the serpent's head will be crushed, and creation restored. So, let us continue this journey, fully aware of the enemy's schemes but even more aware of God's victory.

Chapter 10 - Choice and Consequence: How Free Will Led to the Fall

As the serpent's deception unravels, we find ourselves at the threshold of one of the most pivotal moments in human history—the moment where choice, temptation, and free will converge, setting the course for all that would follow. In Chapter 9, we uncovered the true nature of the nachash, the "shining one," whose manipulation in the Garden of Eden echoed the cosmic rebellion that began with Lucifer. Now, our focus turns to humanity's response, and how the exercise of free will led not only to disobedience but to the fall that would impact every generation to come.

The serpent may have introduced doubt and distorted the truth, but the decision that Adam and Eve faced was entirely their own. The weight of their choice reverberates through time, a powerful reminder of the delicate balance between free will and obedience, between temptation and trust.

The Nature of Free Will: A Divine Gift

Free will is central to the human experience, isn't it? It is one of the most profound gifts that God bestowed upon humanity—an expression of being made in His image. As we explored in Chapter 6, free will isn't just the ability to choose between right and wrong; it's the capacity to engage in a genuine, loving relationship with the Creator. Without free will, love would be mechanical, mere obedience forced by programming. But in granting humanity the freedom to choose, God opened the door to authentic connection—and with it, the risk of rebellion.

God's command in Genesis 2:16-17— "You may surely eat of every tree of the garden, but of the tree of the knowledge of good and evil you shall not eat, for in the day that you eat of it you shall surely die"—established a clear boundary within the covenant relationship between God and humanity. The boundary wasn't arbitrary; it was designed to protect humanity's innocence and trust. Adam and Eve were given the freedom to choose love, trust, and dependence on God, but they were also given the freedom to turn away.

In that choice lay the power to uphold or to break the divine order, and as the serpent whispered his distortions, that choice came sharply into focus.

The Serpent's Subtle Deception

The nachash—the serpent—did not force Eve's hand. Instead, he planted a seed of doubt, twisting the truth just enough to suggest that God's command was meant to restrict rather than protect. "You will not surely die," the serpent told Eve, contradicting God's warning and appealing to her curiosity and desire for wisdom. His words played on her autonomy, suggesting that by eating the fruit, she could gain something God was withholding—knowledge of good and evil.

What's important to realize here is that the serpent's tactic was not an outright lie. Rather, it was a subtle distortion, a manipulation of truth that masked the far-reaching consequences of disobedience. The serpent implied that God's warning wasn't for their good, but rather to keep them from becoming like Him.

In that moment, the narrative shifts. Eve's gaze turns to the fruit, and the seed of doubt begins to grow. Genesis 3:6 describes the fateful moment: "When the woman saw that the tree was good for food, and that it was a delight to the eyes, and that the tree was to be desired to make one wise, she took of its fruit and ate, and she also gave some to her husband who was with her, and he ate."

In a single act, the harmony of creation was broken. The free will that was meant to express love and trust now manifested in disobedience, and the consequences would extend far beyond the garden.

Immediate Consequences: The Disruption of Divine Harmony

The immediate consequence of Adam and Eve's choice was the loss of innocence. The moment their eyes were opened, they became aware of their nakedness—a symbol of vulnerability, shame, and the fracture that had occurred between them and God. Genesis 3:7 describes this sudden realization: "Then the eyes of both were opened, and they knew that they were naked; and they sewed fig leaves together and made themselves loincloths." What was once pure and untainted became stained by disobedience.

But perhaps the most devastating consequence was the rupture in their relationship with God. When they heard the sound of the Lord God walking in the garden, they hid themselves in fear. The intimacy they once shared with their Creator was shattered. Genesis 3:9-10 recounts the chilling exchange: "But the Lord God called to the man and said to him, 'Where are you?' And he said, 'I heard the sound of you in the garden, and I was afraid, because I was naked, and I hid myself.'"

Fear replaced trust. Shame replaced openness. The divine harmony between Creator and creation was now disrupted, and the consequences of this rupture would reverberate throughout human history.

The Continuing Effect of Disobedience

The consequences of Adam and Eve's disobedience did not stop with them. The curse that followed extended to all of creation, fracturing not just human relationships but the very fabric of the world itself.

God's pronouncement in Genesis 3:14-19 outlines the far-reaching effects of their choice:

The Curse on the Serpent: The serpent was cursed to crawl on its belly, signifying both a physical and spiritual fall from its previous exalted state. The enmity between the serpent and humanity was established—a cosmic battle between good and evil that would continue throughout history.

The Curse on the Woman: Eve's curse brought pain into childbirth, a reminder that even the most beautiful aspects of life—bringing forth new life—would now be marked by suffering. The relational dynamic between Adam and Eve would also be affected, introducing tension and struggle into what was meant to be a partnership of love and mutual trust.

The Curse on the Man: For Adam, the ground itself was cursed because of his disobedience. What was once a garden of abundance now becoming a place of toil and frustration. The ground, cursed because of Adam's disobedience, would no longer yield its fruit easily. Thorns and thistles would now characterize the labor required to sustain life, a painful reminder of the cost of rebellion.

These curses represent more than just physical hardships—they symbolize the unraveling of the divine order. The harmony between humanity, creation, and God was broken, and the world would never be the same.

Expulsion from Eden: The Cost of Disobedience

The final consequence of Adam and Eve's disobedience was their expulsion from Eden. The garden, which had been their home and sanctuary, was now closed off to them. Genesis 3:23-24 recounts this heart-wrenching moment: "Therefore the Lord God sent him out from the garden of Eden... He drove out the man, and at the east of the garden of Eden He placed the cherubim and a flaming sword that turned every way to guard the way to the tree of life."

The separation from God's immediate presence was complete. What had been a place of communion was now out of reach, and humanity was left to navigate a world marred by sin, suffering, and separation. This exile from Eden would mark the beginning of a long journey—a journey of redemption that would find its ultimate resolution in the person of Christ.

Theological Reflections: Free Will, Fall, and Redemption

As we reflect on this pivotal moment in the biblical narrative, we are reminded of the delicate balance between free will and consequence. The fall of humanity was not the result of an arbitrary test; it was the natural outcome of the misuse of the very gift that was meant to bring us closer to God. Free will, as we've seen, is both beautiful and dangerous. It allows for love, but it also carries the risk of rebellion.

Yet, even in this tragic story, we find a glimmer of hope. Genesis 3:15, the protoevangelium, speaks of a future victory: "I will put enmity between you and the woman, and between your offspring and her offspring; he shall bruise your head, and you shall bruise his heel." This first promise of redemption points forward to Christ's triumph over the forces of evil, a victory that would reverse the effects of the fall and restore the broken relationship between humanity and God.

A Journey of Redemption

As we continue on this journey, let's not lose sight of the overarching narrative that we've been tracing. The story of humanity's fall is not just about sin and separation; it's about the unfolding plan of redemption. The choices made in the Garden of Eden set in motion a divine drama that would culminate in the life, death, and resurrection of Christ—the ultimate act of love that offers a way back to the light.

In the next chapter, we will explore how the effects of the fall rippled through generations, leading to the moral decline of humanity and the escalating consequences of rebellion. Yet even in the darkest moments, God's redemptive plan remains at the forefront—a promise that no matter how deep the fall, His grace is deeper still.

Genesis 3:23

He drove out the man, and at the east of the garden of Eden he placed the cherubim and a flaming sword that turned every way to guard the way to the tree of life.

Chapter 11 - The Ripple Effect: Moral Decline After Eden

As we look deeper into the early chapters of humanity's history, we witness a tragic narrative of moral decline in the wake of Eden. The harmony of the Garden soon gives way to a world unraveling under the weight of sin. This chapter traces the descent into wrongdoing that ultimately leads to the Great Flood. From the first murder to the distortion of marriage and the rise of idolatry, we will uncover how these events reveal humanity's desperate need for divine intervention and redemption.

The First Murder: Cain and Abel—A Fractured Humanity

The story of Cain and Abel in Genesis 4 provides a sobering glimpse into the rapid moral decay that follows Adam and Eve's disobedience. What began as a choice to eat from the forbidden tree soon spirals into jealousy, murder, and bloodshed. The lives of Cain and Abel illustrate both the far-reaching consequences of sin and the widening rift between humanity and God.

Cain and Abel each offer sacrifices to the Lord—Abel, a shepherd, brings "the firstborn of his flock," while Cain, a farmer, presents "the fruit of the ground" (Genesis 4:3-4). God looks with favor upon Abel's offering, causing Cain to be consumed with jealousy. "Cain was very angry, and his face fell" (Genesis 4:5). In His mercy, God warns Cain, offering him a way to overcome the temptation he faces: "If you do well, will you not be accepted? And if you do not do well, sin is crouching at the door. Its desire is for you, but you must rule over it" (Genesis 4:7).

Tragically, Cain chooses a different path. Rather than mastering his anger, he allows it to consume him, luring Abel into the field and committing the first murder (Genesis 4:8). This act represents the introduction of violence into human relationships, where sin not only separates humanity from God but also turns people against one another. When God confronts Cain with the question, "What have you done? The voice of your brother's blood is crying to me from the ground" (Genesis 4:10), it is a stark reminder that sin disrupts not only human relationships but creation itself.

Cain's Consequences: Restlessness and Alienation

Cain's punishment is swift. He is condemned to wander the earth, severed from the land he once cultivated: "When you work the ground, it shall no longer yield to you, its strength. You shall be a fugitive and a wanderer" (Genesis 4:12). Despite his judgment, God shows mercy by placing a protective mark on Cain, declaring, "If anyone kills Cain, vengeance shall be taken on him sevenfold" (Genesis 4:15). Cain's life becomes one of restlessness and alienation, embodying the disconnection that sin brings.

A World Spiraling into Violence

Cain's defiant question— "Am I my brother's keeper?"—echoes throughout Scripture as a symbol of humanity's growing disregard for moral responsibility. From Esau and Jacob to Joseph and his brothers, we see a recurring theme of fractured relationships and brotherly conflict, all stemming from the root of sin.

Lamech, a descendant of Cain, intensifies this cycle of violence. He brazenly boasts of killing a man for wounding him (Genesis 4:23), taking pride in his act of vengeance. What began with Cain's individual sin now blossoms into a culture of bloodshed and revenge, pulling humanity further from God's original design.

Yet, amidst this spiral of corruption, there is a glimmer of hope. Adam and Eve's third son, Seth, signals a new beginning. His lineage "calls upon the name of the Lord" (Genesis 4:26), offering a contrast to Cain's violent descendants. This division between Cain's line of violence and Seth's faithful lineage sets the stage for the unfolding narrative of moral decline and the judgment to come.

Lamech's Rebellion: Corruption of Marriage and Morality

Lamech's defiance extends beyond violence—he also distorts the divine institution of marriage. By taking two wives (Genesis 4:19), Lamech rejects God's design for monogamy as established in Eden (Genesis 2:24). This rejection of God's covenant further deepens the moral corruption spreading through humanity.

His pride in violence and disregard for God's guidelines symbolize a broader moral decay that infects society. As human beings turn further away from God's design, the consequences of sin continue to ripple through generations.

The Rise of Idolatry and Widespread Corruption

As humanity multiplies, so too does its moral degradation. By the time of Noah, the earth is described as "filled with violence" and "corrupt in God's sight" (Genesis 6:11-12). The wickedness of humanity reaches a devastating peak: "The intentions of the thoughts of their hearts were only evil continually" (Genesis 6:5).

Idolatry becomes rampant as people abandon the Creator and craft gods of their own making. "They exchanged the glory of the immortal God for images" (Romans 1:23), trading truth for lies. This idolatry fuels deeper ethical chaos, unraveling the moral fabric of societies that had once adhered to divine principles.

As corruption spreads, God prepares for judgment. But amid the moral darkness, there remains a thread of hope—a cry for redemption that will find expression in the story of Noah.

Genesis 4:10-11

And the Lord said, "What have you done? The voice of your brother's blood is crying to me from the ground. And now you are cursed from the ground, which has opened its mouth to receive your brother's blood from your hand.

Chapter 12 - The Heavenly Rebellion: Fall of the sons of God

Have you ever paused to reflect on the spiritual battles that unfold not only in our world but also in the heavens above? The rebellion that began in the Garden of Eden is part of a much larger cosmic conflict—a struggle that transcends human experience and extends into the spiritual realm. In this chapter, we'll explore the fateful choices made by the "Sons of God," celestial beings whose defiance of their Creator unleashed chaos upon the earth. Their rebellion, which led to the rise of the Nephilim, deepened humanity's moral decline and pushed the world to a pivotal moment in history. While it is a weighty narrative, it is crucial to understanding the broader spiritual struggle that runs through the Bible.

The Sons of God: Different Perspectives

The identity of the "Sons of God" in Genesis 6 has sparked debate for centuries. Scholars and theologians have proposed various interpretations, but two main views dominate the discussion—the Sethite view and the Royalty view—both of which offer human-centered explanations but ultimately fall short of capturing the full theological depth of the text.

The Sethite view suggests that the "Sons of God" were descendants of Seth, the righteous line, who intermarried with the "daughters of men," assumed to be descendants of Cain. This interpretation, however, overlooks the supernatural context of the phrase "Sons of God." In Scripture, the term consistently refers to divine beings, as seen in Job 1:6 and Job 38:7. Moreover, the idea that intermarriage between two human lineages could result in the Nephilim—beings of extraordinary size and strength—raises questions that the Sethite interpretation cannot fully address.

The Royalty view posits that the "Sons of God" were kings or rulers who flaunted their power through polygamy and abuse of authority. While it is true that many ancient rulers considered themselves divine or semi-divine, this explanation fails to account for the clear supernatural elements in the Genesis 6 narrative. It also doesn't explain why the Nephilim—"the mighty men of old"—would arise from these unions.

Both interpretations fall short because they ignore the deeper, cosmic implications of Genesis 6—a chapter that points to the battle between divine beings and humanity, setting the stage for much of the Bible's spiritual narrative. The term "Sons of God" points to divine beings—angels—who abandoned their rightful place. Jude 1:6 and 2 Peter 2:4 reinforce this interpretation, describing angels who "did not stay within their own position of authority, but left their proper dwelling." This understanding not only fits the text but also explains the cosmic scale of the rebellion that led to divine judgment. By seeing the Sons of God as fallen angels, we gain a fuller appreciation for the gravity of their actions and their role in human history.

The Choice to Rebel: Desire, Power, and a Break from Divine Order

In Genesis 6:1-4, we encounter a sobering narrative: "When human beings began to multiply on the face of the land, and daughters were born to them, the Sons of God saw that the daughters of man were attractive. And they took as their wives any they chose." This was not a mere violation of human customs; it was a profound act of rebellion against God's divine order. By crossing the boundary between the heavenly and earthly realms, the Sons of God defied their Creator and pursued their own desires.

What drove these celestial beings to abandon their rightful place? Their rebellion wasn't only about desire—it was about power. They sought autonomy, an ambition to reshape their existence outside of God's will.

This mirrors the same temptation that lured Satan and later ensnared Adam and Eve: the desire to grasp autonomy and control outside of God's established boundaries. As we explored in Chapter 4, Satan's fall was driven by a similar thirst for self-exaltation, and here we see a parallel among the Sons of God.

The consequences of their rebellion were catastrophic. The Nephilim, "the mighty men of old," were born from the union of the Sons of God and human women. These beings symbolized the distortion of God's creation—a blending of the spiritual and physical realms that introduced chaos into the world. This act of rebellion parallels humanity's fall and deepens the corruption on earth, as we saw in Chapter 8 with the serpent's deception. The desire to defy divine order always leads to destruction—a truth that echoes throughout the biblical narrative.

Mount Hermon: A Symbol of Rebellion

Certain locations in Scripture carry deep spiritual significance, and Mount Hermon is one such place—a site steeped in the theme of rebellion. According to the Book of Enoch, Mount Hermon was where the Sons of God descended to earth, binding themselves in an oath to rebel against God. While the Book of Enoch is not part of the biblical canon, it provides valuable historical and theological context. Interestingly, both Jude 1:14-15 and 2 Peter 2:4 reference events that are also found in Enoch, indicating that early Christians, including the apostles, were familiar with its content and saw it as a source of insight into these spiritual matters.

Mount Hermon, originally a symbol of divine majesty, became a focal point of cosmic defiance. Once celebrated for its beauty and height—as mentioned in Psalm 133:3, where the "dew of Hermon" symbolizes blessing—its legacy became tarnished by rebellion. By the time of Jesus, the region near Hermon, particularly Caesarea Philippi, had become associated with pagan worship and spiritual darkness. Jesus' declaration near this very region— "the gates of hell shall not prevail against it" (Matthew 16:18)—was a direct challenge to the entrenched spiritual rebellion that had long been tied to the mountain.

Mount Hermon reminds us of a critical spiritual truth: rebellion against God's order, whether in the heavens or on earth, has far-reaching consequences. But even in the darkest places, God's sovereignty and redemptive plan remain unshaken.

Satan's Role in the Rebellion

Although Satan is not explicitly named in Genesis 6, his influence is unmistakable. The rebellion of the Sons of God reflects the same pride and ambition that characterized Satan's fall. As we explored in Chapter 5, Satan's desire to "ascend above" God in Isaiah 14:12-15 set the pattern for cosmic defiance. The Sons of God, in abandoning their divine roles, followed in his footsteps, seeking power and control apart from God's design.

But what does this pattern reveal? Satan's rebellion in the spiritual realm set the stage for the Sons of God to reject their rightful place, just as his temptation of Adam and Eve set humanity on a path toward moral decay. Their actions were not isolated events but part of the larger cosmic battle that began with Satan's rebellion and continues to ripple through history.

This recurring pattern of rebellion against divine order highlights the spiritual warfare that underpins the biblical narrative. The consequences of these cosmic rebellions—both Satan's and the Sons of God's—profoundly affected both the spiritual and physical realms. Yet, amid the darkness, God's plan for redemption remains, offering hope for a world corrupted by sin.

Jude 1:6

And the angels who did not stay within their own position of authority, but left their proper dwelling,

Origins of Disobedience

Numbers 13:33

And there we saw the Nephilim
(the sons of Anak, who come from the Nephilim),
and we seemed to ourselves like grasshoppers,
and so we seemed to them.

Chapter 13 - Giants Among Us: The Nephilim and Their Legacy

Have you ever considered how one act of rebellion can send ripples across not only a lifetime but through all of creation? The story of the Nephilim, the hybrid race born from the defiance of the Sons of God, offers profound insights into how spiritual rebellion can shape the course of history. These giants were not merely physical anomalies; they were embodiments of moral corruption and chaos, twisting the divine order and leading humanity deeper into disarray. As we explore the rise of the Nephilim, the forbidden knowledge they imparted, and the echoes of their legacy today, we uncover a cautionary tale of what happens when boundaries set by God are disregarded.

The Nephilim: A Result of Rebellion

The Nephilim's origins are directly tied to the rebellion of the Sons of God, detailed in Genesis 6:1-4. These celestial beings, drawn by lust for human women, crossed divine boundaries and birthed a hybrid race that forever altered human history. "The Nephilim were on the earth in those days, and also afterward, when the sons of God came in to the daughters of man and they bore children to them. These were the mighty men who were of old, the men of renown" (Genesis 6:4). This was no ordinary union; it was an act of rebellion that fractured the natural and spiritual worlds, leading to immense chaos and violence.

The term "Nephilim" is often interpreted as "giants," but its root, naphal, also means "fallen ones," hinting at both their towering stature and their spiritual corruption. Their legacy as "men of renown" is a chilling reminder that their power and influence were rooted not in righteousness, but in domination, warfare, and the defilement of humanity. As scholar Michael Heiser notes in The Unseen Realm, the

Nephilim stand as a physical and spiritual manifestation of rebellion—a literal and figurative fall from grace.

Yet, as we contemplate the Nephilim, it's important to remember that they were more than giants in the physical sense. They represented a deeper corruption, a blending of divine and human that violated the boundaries of creation. This single act of defiance set off a cascade of chaos, drawing humanity further away from God's design—a pattern of disobedience that, as we've seen in previous chapters, is echoed throughout Scripture.

Forbidden Knowledge: A Catalyst for Chaos

One of the most devastating consequences of the Nephilim's existence was the forbidden knowledge they, along with their fallen spiritual fathers, imparted to humanity. This knowledge—ranging from the crafting of weapons to the practice of sorcery and enchantments—profoundly altered the course of human history. What had once been a world built on communal harmony and mutual care was now thrown into disarray, as tools of peace were turned into instruments of violence and power.

As we noted in the previous chapter, while the Book of Enoch is not part of the biblical canon, it was highly regarded during the intertestamental period and remains an invaluable resource for understanding the spiritual and cultural context of early Jewish thought. Both Jude (1:14-15) and Peter (2 Peter 2:4) reference events from Enoch, affirming its influence in shedding light on the spiritual realities of that time. In 1 Enoch (8:1-3), it is revealed that these fallen beings taught humanity the art of forging swords, knives, shields, and armor—turning a peaceful world into one dominated by conflict and bloodshed.

The introduction of weapons into a society once defined by cooperation drastically changed the trajectory of human civilization.

Tools meant for defense and survival became tools of aggression and conquest. Genesis 6:11 vividly captures the result: "Now the earth was corrupt in God's sight, and the earth was filled with violence." With this forbidden knowledge came a cultural shift, where power, dominance, and brute force became the new values by which society operated.

But the impact went far beyond physical violence. The Nephilim, originally creatures that should have adhered to divine order, instead became agents of chaos and destruction. They introduced a twisted ideology where might triumphed over morality, and strength became the measure of right. The corruption they spread seeped into the very fabric of human relationships, leading to widespread conflict, oppression, and the eventual need for God's direct intervention to restore order to His creation.

The Nephilim's Role in the Great Flood

The rise of the Nephilim and their corrupting influence is a key factor in the unfolding narrative that leads to the Great Flood. These hybrids, born of rebellion, blurred the lines between the divine and human realms and introduced an unprecedented level of violence and depravity into the world. Their actions, combined with the moral decay of humanity, prompted God's heart-wrenching decision to cleanse the earth.

Genesis 6:5-7 reveals God's deep sorrow over the state of His creation: "The LORD saw that the wickedness of man was great in the earth, and that every intention of the thoughts of his heart was only evil continually. And the LORD regretted that he had made man on the earth, and it grieved him to his heart." The presence of the Nephilim and the devastation they caused made this divine judgment necessary.

Yet, as severe as the flood was, it was not merely an act of destruction—it was also an act of redemption. God's decision to cleanse the world through the flood was not just a punishment but a reset, an opportunity to restore creation to its intended order. Noah, described as "a righteous man, blameless in his generation" (Genesis 6:9), was chosen as the remnant through which humanity would continue—a flicker of hope in a world overwhelmed by chaos.

The Disembodied Spirits: A Haunting Legacy

The physical destruction of the Nephilim may have occurred with the flood, but their legacy continued in the form of their disembodied spirits. According to ancient Jewish tradition and early Christian writings, these spirits became the malevolent entities we now recognize as demons—spirits that still torment and lead humanity astray.

While the celestial beings who fathered the Nephilim were bound in chains awaiting final judgment (Jude 1:6, 2 Peter 2:4), the spirits of the Nephilim were left to roam the earth, furthering the rebellion they had been born into. In The Book of Enoch, these spirits are referred to as "evil spirits" or "bastard spirits," and they continue their influence by tempting and deceiving humans, fostering moral decay and rebellion against God.

Their continued presence is a reminder of the lasting consequences of spiritual rebellion. What began as an act of defiance in the heavenly realms continues to reverberate through human history, influencing hearts and minds even today. These spirits, separated from their physical forms, now seek to perpetuate the chaos their forefathers introduced into the world.

The Ongoing Legacy of the Nephilim

As we prepare to look deeper into the flood and its aftermath, we must recognize that the flood was not only an act of judgment but an act of divine mercy. God's covenant with Noah represents His ongoing commitment to His creation, offering humanity a second chance to live within His boundaries. The physical presence of the Nephilim may have been wiped away, but the spiritual battle rages on.

The legacy of the Nephilim serves as a sobering reminder of the far-reaching effects of rebellion. Though they were destroyed physically, their influence persists in the spiritual realm. Their disembodied spirits continue to wage war against humanity, undermining God's order and drawing people away from His truth. Yet, even in the face of this persistent rebellion, God's plan for redemption remains steadfast.

As we move forward in our journey, let's hold onto the hope that God's purpose for creation is one of restoration. The flood may have been a necessary judgment, but it also cleared the path for renewal—a chance to begin again under God's covenant promises. Together, we will explore how this act of cleansing led to a new chapter in human history, and how the legacy of the Nephilim, while haunting, points us toward a future where righteousness will prevail.

Genesis 7:6-7

Noah was six hundred years old when the flood of waters came upon the earth. And Noah and his sons and his wife and his sons' wives with him went into the ark to escape the waters of the flood.

Chapter 14 - Waters of Judgment: The Flood's Purging Power

Have you ever considered just how far human corruption can go—and what lengths divine justice may take to restore order? The story of the Flood is a powerful testament to God's response when humanity strays too far from His intended design. It is a narrative intertwined with themes of creation, rebellion, judgment, and, ultimately, the hope of renewal. What was once declared "very good" (Genesis 1:31) had descended into violence, wickedness, and chaos. The unholy union between divine beings and human women unleashed forbidden knowledge, dragging humanity deeper into sin. In response, God resolved to cleanse the earth through the Flood—a dramatic act of both judgment and mercy, aimed at erasing corruption and giving creation a fresh start.

A World Consumed by Evil

Imagine a world where every thought and intention is steeped in evil, where creation itself has become warped beyond recognition. Genesis 6:5 paints this tragic picture: "The Lord saw that the wickedness of man was great in the earth, and that every intention of the thoughts of his heart was only evil continually." This is the culmination of human rebellion—a rebellion that began with Adam and Eve and spiraled into something far more destructive with the influence of the fallen "sons of God."

As explored in the previous chapter, these divine beings crossed a sacred boundary, their union with human women producing the Nephilim—giant, powerful beings who symbolized humanity's increasing descent into chaos. They were not just physical giants but figures of domination, influencing the world through violence and the distortion of God's design for creation. They represent a world gripped by the hunger for power, consumed by violence, and utterly out of alignment with God's original purpose.

God's grief over this corruption is profoundly expressed in Genesis 6:6: "And the Lord regretted that he had made man on the earth, and it grieved him to his heart." This is not the regret of a distant, dispassionate deity; it is the sorrow of a Creator who watches His beloved creation rebel against Him. The deep personal grief of God reveals the relational aspect of humanity's rebellion—turning away from God is not just an act of defiance; it breaks the heart of the One who made us.

A Flood of Judgment and Mercy

God's decision to send the Flood is not a knee-jerk reaction to humanity's wickedness—it is a deliberate act of justice designed to restore order to a world gone awry. Genesis 6:7 records His solemn declaration: "I will blot out man whom I have created from the face of the land... for I am sorry that I have made them." The Flood was not just about punishing humanity; it was a reset, a way to re-establish divine order in a world drowning in chaos. It was a purging, a cleansing, aimed at sweeping away the moral decay that had infiltrated every corner of creation.

The Nephilim, along with the rebellious angels who had abandoned their heavenly roles, were at the heart of this corruption. Their influence had permeated human society, leading to violence, oppression, and the loss of God's original design for the earth. The Flood became the necessary response to this unrestrained rebellion—a way to eradicate both the Nephilim and the spiritual forces behind them, who had sought to exploit humanity for their own purposes.

Yet, in this act of judgment, we must also recognize the presence of mercy. God's aim was not to destroy for destruction's sake, but to cleanse so that renewal could begin. The Flood was not the end of the story, but the beginning of something new. By preserving Noah and his family, God ensured that His covenant with humanity and creation could continue, even in the face of overwhelming wickedness.

The Cleansing Waters: Judgment Rewrites Creation

In unleashing the Flood, God released the waters that once sustained life, now to cleanse the earth of its corruption. As discussed in earlier chapters, the pre-Flood world was likely protected by a water vapor canopy that fostered a temperate climate and long lifespans. When this canopy was ruptured, rain poured down from the heavens while subterranean waters burst forth from the earth. Genesis 7:11 describes this moment vividly: "The fountains of the great deep burst forth, and the windows of the heavens were opened."

The elements that once nurtured life now became instruments of divine cleansing. The waters rose and covered the earth, submerging not only the Nephilim and their corruption but also the entire world that had embraced wickedness. Through this act, God demonstrated His unwavering resolve to confront sin—transforming the waters that once gave life into agents of judgment.

Amid this deluge, Noah and his family found refuge in the ark. Built according to God's precise instructions, the ark became a vessel of hope, a symbol of both judgment and salvation. While the world outside was submerged in chaos, inside the ark, God's plan for a restored creation remained alive. This contrast between destruction and protection shows God's dual purposes in the Flood: to cleanse, but also to preserve a faithful remnant who would carry forward His vision for a renewed earth.

A New Beginning: Hope Through Judgment

As the floodwaters receded, the earth emerged cleansed, ready for renewal. Genesis 7:23 declares: "He blotted out every living thing that was on the face of the ground… Only Noah was left, and those who were with him in the ark." The Nephilim—who had embodied rebellion, corruption, and violence—were no more. The rebellious angels, too, were judged and cast down, their influence removed from the world they had sought to dominate.

The Flood achieved its purpose: it washed away the corruption that had tainted creation, making way for a fresh start. But this judgment was not the final word—it was the gateway to restoration. God's preservation of Noah and his family signifies His desire for humanity to return to a place of righteousness, to walk in harmony with His will. Through Noah, a new chapter in human history began, one grounded in the promise of renewal.

In this act of judgment, we see both the severity of God's justice and the depths of His mercy. The Flood was not an end, but a new beginning—a world washed clean, ready for God's covenant with Noah and the unfolding of His redemptive plan.

Looking Ahead: The Covenant of Renewal

As we move forward, the Flood stands as a pivotal moment—a moment where judgment and mercy intersect. The world has been cleansed, and now God will establish His covenant with Noah, a covenant that carries the promise of renewal and the hope of redemption.

In the next chapter, we will explore the covenant God makes with Noah after the Flood. This covenant marks a turning point in God's relationship with humanity, offering a promise that echoes throughout Scripture—a promise that despite humanity's failures, God's plan for restoration remains steadfast.

Genesis 7:23

He blotted out every living thing that was on the face of the ground, man and animals and creeping things and birds of the heavens. They were blotted out from the earth. Only Noah was left, and those who were with him in the ark.

Genesis 9:14-15

When I bring clouds over the earth and the bow is seen in the clouds, I will remember my covenant that is between me and you and every living creature of all flesh.
And the waters shall never again become a flood to destroy all flesh.

Chapter 15 - After the Waters:
The Return of Sin and Roots of Rebellion

Have you ever felt the flicker of hope that comes with a fresh start, only to sense the weight of familiar failures creeping back in? I know I have. After the Flood, humanity was given an extraordinary opportunity—a divine reset that washed away the grotesque manifestations of evil in both the physical and spiritual realms. With the Nephilim destroyed and the rebellious Sons of God judged, Noah and his family stepped into a world that should have been pure, a world renewed. Yet, as we look back on the course of history, we see a harsh reality: the heart of humanity remained unchanged. Sin, washed away in one form, quickly found a way to reemerge.

In this chapter, we'll take a closer look at the resurgence of sin after the Flood. We'll explore the curse of Canaan, the rebellious lineage of Ham, and how these roots of defiance ultimately led to Nimrod, ushering in a new phase of human rebellion against God.

The Opportunity for Restoration

After the Flood, God extended to Noah and his family a profound promise of new beginnings. The covenant He established, symbolized by the rainbow, was more than just a reassurance; it was an invitation to rebuild and restore what had been irrevocably lost in Eden. Can you feel the weight of that promise? "Never again shall there be a flood to destroy the earth" (Genesis 9:11)—this was not only a divine guarantee but also a call to responsibility and renewal.

In this new world, Noah's blessing echoed God's original command to Adam: "Be fruitful and multiply, and fill the earth" (Genesis 9:1). This mandate reaffirmed humanity's role as stewards of creation. Yet beneath the surface of this hope, sin lay dormant, waiting to sprout at the first opportunity. While the Flood had removed the visible manifestations of wickedness, it had not transformed the internal condition of the human heart. The rebellion that had once corrupted the pre-Flood world wasn't eradicated, only postponed.

As we reflect on the stories that have unfolded so far, we see that while the opportunity for restoration existed, the human struggle with sin remained. Isn't that a struggle we can all relate to? How often have we found ourselves falling back into old habits, despite our best intentions? This is the shared human condition—a cycle of hope and disappointment, of renewal and failure.

The Curse of Canaan: Ham's Sin and Its Consequences

The first signs of sin's return appeared disturbingly close to home, within Noah's own family. After planting a vineyard, Noah became intoxicated and lay uncovered in his tent (Genesis 9:20-21). Even in the most righteous of people, moments of vulnerability exist. Ham, one of Noah's sons, happened upon the scene and dishonored his father by exposing Noah's shame to his brothers rather than covering it (Genesis 9:22). His actions revealed not just a failure of respect but a deeper disregard for divine order.

When Noah awoke and learned of Ham's actions, he pronounced a curse—not upon Ham, but upon Canaan, Ham's son: "Cursed be Canaan; a servant of servants shall he be to his brothers" (Genesis 9:25). This curse would echo throughout generations, foreshadowing future conflicts between Canaan's descendants and the Israelites. More than simple retribution, this curse illustrates a core biblical principle: the consequences of sin can transcend individuals, reaching into future generations and affecting entire communities.

The curse on Canaan was more than a family conflict—it revealed the deep, ongoing struggle against defiance of God's order. Ham's dishonor marked the beginning of a lineage shaped by rebellion, embedding the roots of sin deeply into the family line. Reflecting on this, I can't help but wonder about our own actions. How often do our decisions ripple outward, affecting those we love, sometimes in ways we can't foresee? It's a sobering reminder that our choices carry weight—weight that can feel heavier than we ever imagined.

The Lineage of Ham: The Birth of Rebellion Through Cush and Nimrod

Ham's descendants, particularly through his son Cush, play a critical role in the post-Flood world. Cush fathered Nimrod, a figure whose legacy is both monumental and deeply troubling. Genesis 10:8-9 describes him as "the first on earth to be a mighty man... a mighty hunter before the Lord." But his might wasn't merely physical; it was rooted in a desire for power and autonomy—a direct challenge to divine authority.

Nimrod's ambitions led him to establish key cities, including Babel, Erech, Akkad, and Calneh, in the land of Shinar (Genesis 10:10). His endeavors reflected a collective human aspiration to create a society independent of God. The name "Nimrod" is often associated with rebellion, thought to mean "we shall rebel." His most infamous project, the construction of the Tower of Babel, stands as a powerful symbol of human pride and defiance. The people sought to "make a name for ourselves" (Genesis 11:4), directly opposing God's command to spread across the earth and multiply.

The Tower of Babel became a monument to humanity's enduring desire to usurp divine authority—a spiritual continuation of the rebellion that had characterized the pre-Flood world. Nimrod's actions reveal a profound truth: when humanity is given a second chance, we often choose power and self-exaltation over righteousness and restoration. This sets a new paradigm of rebellion that resonates through the ages, illustrating the complex interplay between divine authority and human ambition.

Sin's Return and the Lingering Darkness

Despite the promise of restoration following the Flood, humanity's propensity for sin reasserted itself almost immediately. Ham's dishonor and the curse upon Canaan were just the beginning. The human heart, unchanged, still gravitated toward rebellion and defiance. Noah's drunkenness and Ham's mockery illustrate how swiftly sin can infiltrate even the most righteous of families. This act of dishonor set a precedent for a lineage marked by conflict and moral decay—a lineage that would ultimately give rise to Nimrod.

As the generations unfolded, Ham's descendants continued to embody opposition against God, epitomized in Nimrod. His rise as a mighty hunter and city-builder symbolized humanity's determination to establish legacies independent of divine guidance. His ambition would eventually culminate in the construction of the Tower of Babel, a bold statement of human defiance against divine authority. The aspiration to "make a name for ourselves" echoed the pride that had led to humanity's previous downfall, revealing an enduring desire for self-aggrandizement that would pave the way for future rebellion.

The Tower of Babel stands as a towering testament to human ambition, encapsulating a profound shift from divine purpose to self-serving endeavors. Rather than fulfilling God's command to spread across the earth, humanity sought to consolidate power, establishing a singular identity and rejecting the natural order God had set in place. This monumental act of rebellion invited divine intervention, leading to the confounding of languages and the scattering of people across the earth. Yet, even though this judgment didn't eradicate sin; it merely diversified its expressions as different cultures and nations formed, many of which embraced their own forms of idolatry and defiance.

Ultimately, the post-Flood narrative serves as a sobering reminder that sin's pervasive nature is inescapable. The struggle against inherent wickedness didn't end with the Flood; rather, it transformed, taking on new shapes and forms as humanity carved its own paths apart from

God. As the threads of rebellion wove through the tapestry of history, they illustrated a profound truth: humanity's quest for autonomy often leads to conflict, division, and moral decay.

The Roots of Rebellion and the Challenge of Restoration

Despite the physical cleansing of the Flood, the post-Flood world remained trapped in spiritual and moral failure. The curse upon Canaan served as a stark reminder of the consequences of rebellion against God's order. It is in this context that Nimrod emerges as a central figure, embodying humanity's relentless drive toward defiance.

As we transition to the next chapter, "Tower of Defiance: Babel and the Disinheritance of the Nations," we will explore how this monumental act of human pride led to the fragmentation of languages and the scattering of nations. This event reflects a broader theme of divine disinheritance, laying the groundwork for future conflicts and the ongoing tension between divine authority and human ambition.

Yet, even amid this judgment, God's redemptive plan continues to take shape. The division of languages and nations did not signify the end of God's relationship with humanity; instead, it marked a pivotal moment in His ongoing narrative of restoration. God's commitment to reclaim His creation becomes evident as He initiates a covenant with Abraham, promising to bless all nations through him (Genesis 12:3). Through Israel—and ultimately through Jesus Christ—the promise of redemption weaves through the fabric of Scripture, inviting us to recognize our need for reconciliation with the Creator.

In this intricate tapestry of sin, judgment, and hope, we find the enduring promise of restoration echoing through the ages. The story of Nimrod, Babel, and the legacy of Ham serves as a powerful reminder of our shared struggle and the ever-present grace of God that calls us back into relationship with Him.

Genesis 10: 9-10

He was a mighty hunter before the Lord. Therefore, it is said, "Like Nimrod a mighty hunter before the Lord."

Chapter 16 - Reaching for Heaven:
Babel's Pride, Disinheritance of the Nations

Imagine a world brimming with promise—a fresh start for humanity after the Flood, where the scars of sin could be healed and a new chapter could be written. The air carried the fragrance of renewal, and the possibility of re-establishing a divine connection felt palpable. Yet, this hope, like a flickering flame, was quickly overshadowed by humanity's unrelenting pride and rebellion. Instead of embracing God's plan, people pursued their own paths, and at the heart of this defiance stood Nimrod—a figure whose ambition ignited a rebellion against God's authority.

Nimrod's vision led to the construction of the Tower of Babel, a symbol of human arrogance that defied God's command to "fill the earth" (Genesis 9:1). In this chapter, we'll explore Nimrod's rise to power, the monumental tower he inspired, its connection to the ziggurat Etemenanki in Babylon, and the spiritual implications of these towering structures as gateways to lesser gods. Ultimately, we'll see how God's swift judgment at Babel scattered the nations, marking a pivotal moment in the unfolding story of divine redemption.

Nimrod's Ambition and the Rise of Babel

Nimrod, the great-grandson of Noah through Ham, first emerges in Genesis 10 as a powerful and charismatic leader—a "mighty hunter before the Lord" who established key cities in the land of Shinar, including Babel. But Nimrod's story goes deeper than his skill as a hunter or city-builder. His ambition was more than just political; it was spiritual. Rather than dispersing and filling the earth as God had commanded (Genesis 9:1), Nimrod sought to centralize power, gathering people into one place in direct defiance of God's plan.

This rebellion wasn't just a political maneuver; it was an echo of humanity's deeper struggle against divine authority—a defiance that traces back to the Garden of Eden. Nimrod's desire to consolidate power and resist God's command mirrors the ongoing battle between human autonomy and divine will. His story is a reminder of how easily we, too, can be tempted to prioritize our own ambitions over our relationship with God.

The Tower of Babel was more than a mere construction project; it was a monument to human pride. As Genesis 11:4 records, the people proclaimed, "Come, let us build ourselves a city and a tower with its top in the heavens, and let us make a name for ourselves." This wasn't just a desire to build something grand; it was an attempt to reach the heavens on their own terms, rejecting their dependence on God. Their actions reflected a deep desire for self-exaltation, a desire that echoed Lucifer's fall when he sought to ascend above the clouds and rival God (Isaiah 14:14).

The Ziggurat Etemenanki: Babel as a Gateway to the Gods

To fully understand the spiritual significance of Babel, we need to look at the connection to the ziggurat Etemenanki in Babylon. Ziggurats were towering structures, like stepped pyramids, built to bridge the gap between the divine and human realms. Etemenanki, which means "temple of the foundation of heaven and earth," was one such structure—a massive ziggurat that stood in the heart of Babylon. Its purpose wasn't merely architectural; it symbolized humanity's desire to ascend to the heavens and interact with the divine on their terms.

Can you picture it? A monumental structure reaching into the sky, its base firmly planted on the earth, its pinnacle stretching toward the heavens. The ziggurat stood as a declaration of human ambition and spiritual desire. The people of Babel weren't content to trust God to reach down to them; they wanted to build a stairway to heaven, a pathway to the gods they could control. But the Tower of Babel was not just an architectural feat—it was a spiritual rebellion, a challenge to God's authority, as if humanity could establish its own divine connection apart from God.

The connection between Babel and the ziggurats like Etemenanki highlights humanity's deep-seated desire to transcend its earthly existence, but also its propensity to do so in defiance of God's order. These structures were intended as gateways for gods to descend and communicate with humans, but in doing so, they reflected a dangerous shift—an idolatrous attempt to manipulate the divine for human purposes. This longing for control, this desire to build our own paths to the heavens, remains a theme that echoes throughout history.

The Tower of Babel stands as a cautionary tale, reminding us of our own tendencies to construct our "towers"—those ambitions or achievements we pursue, believing they will elevate us, often at the expense of our relationship with God. But no matter how high we build, without God at the center, we are simply stacking bricks of pride and rebellion.

The Judgment of Babel: Scattering and Disinheritance

The story of Babel is more than just a tale of architectural ambition; it represents humanity's collective attempt to dethrone God and establish its authority. As people gathered under Nimrod's leadership to build the tower, they sought more than physical heights—they were striving for spiritual independence. This was the same spirit of rebellion that had marked humanity since Eden, the same desire to be "like God," to define good and evil on their own terms.

God saw the heart of their rebellion and intervened, not out of anger, but out of a deep understanding of where such unchecked pride would lead. In Genesis 11:6, God says, "Behold, they are one people, and they all have one language, and this is only the beginning of what they will do." God recognized that if humanity continued in this unified rebellion, the consequences would be catastrophic. And so, He confused their language, scattering them across the earth. What had once been a unified ambition dissolved into chaos.

But this scattering was more than just a disruption of their plans; it marked a profound spiritual event—what theologians refer to as the disinheritance of the nations. According to Deuteronomy 32:8-9, God divided the nations and handed them over to the rule of lesser divine beings—spiritual entities who would govern them in place of the direct relationship humanity once enjoyed with God. While these nations were disinherited, God reserved one nation for Himself—Israel. Through this chosen people, God would begin His redemptive plan to reclaim humanity from the grip of rebellion.

The judgment of Babel wasn't simply about scattering people across the earth; it was a response to humanity's prideful attempt to bypass God. Yet even in judgment, God's mercy was evident. Though the nations were scattered and handed over to lesser powers, God's ultimate plan was always one of restoration. Through Israel—and ultimately through Jesus—God would begin the process of reclaiming the nations for Himself.

Reflection and Transition: From Rebellion to Redemption

The Tower of Babel invites us to reflect on our own hearts. How often do we, like the people of Babel, seek to build our own towers—structures of ambition, pride, or independence that distract us from our dependence on God? Babel teaches us that no matter how grand our efforts, when we build apart from God, we build on shaky ground.

Yet, even in our rebellion, God's grace remains. The scattering of Babel wasn't the end of the story; it was the beginning of a grand narrative of redemption. Though the nations were disinherited, God set in motion a plan to reclaim them. Through Israel, God would bless the nations, and through Jesus, He would fulfill the promise to unite all people under His kingdom.

As we transition into the next chapter, "Tower of Defiance: Babel and the Disinheritance of the Nations," we'll see how God's plan for redemption begins to take shape. The scattering at Babel led to the division of nations, but it also laid the groundwork for the covenant with Abraham—the beginning of God's promise to bless all peoples of the earth.

Babel may have represented a moment of rebellion and disinheritance, but through God's redemptive plan, what was once divided will one day be restored. The story of Babel is, in the end, a story of hope—a reminder that even when we stray, God is always working to bring us back into relationship with Him.

Let's continue this journey together, as we explore how God's promises to Abraham would set the stage for the ultimate redemption of all nations. No matter how far we stray, His grace is always there, calling us back to the foundation He's laid for us.

Deuteronomy 32:7-9

Remember the days of old; consider the years of many generations; ask your father, and he will show you, your elders, and they will tell you. When the Most High gave to the nations their inheritance, when he divided mankind, he fixed the borders of the peoples according to the number of the sons of God. But the Lord's portion is his people, Jacob his allotted heritage.

Chapter 17 - Divided Lands: The Nations and Their Divine Rulers

Imagine a world brimming with new possibilities—a fresh canvas for humanity after the Flood, painted with the vibrant colors of hope and renewal. The air was alive with the promise of a new beginning, where people could reconnect with their Creator and live in harmony with His design. But like a flickering candle that can be easily snuffed out, that hope was soon overshadowed by the pride and rebellion rooted deep in the human heart. Leading this defiance was Nimrod, an ambitious leader whose actions sparked a profound rebellion against God's intentions, culminating in the construction of the Tower of Babel.

In this chapter, we will explore Nimrod's rise to power, the monumental tower he inspired, and its connections to the ziggurat Etemenanki in Babylon—symbols of humanity's overreaching ambition. We'll also delve into the spiritual significance of these towering structures, which were seen as gateways to lesser gods. Ultimately, we'll see how God's swift judgment at Babel not only scattered the nations but also set the stage for His redemptive plan.

Nimrod's Ambition and the Rise of Babel

Nimrod, the great-grandson of Noah through Ham, is first introduced in Genesis 10 as a "mighty hunter before the Lord"—a figure of immense strength and influence. But Nimrod's ambitions extended far beyond being a skilled hunter. His true legacy was his ability to unify people and consolidate power, founding cities like Babel, Erech, Akkad, and Calneh in the land of Shinar. While on the surface, his leadership may have seemed impressive, Nimrod's ambition wasn't aligned with God's will. Instead of encouraging people to spread out and fill the earth, as God had commanded (Genesis 9:1), Nimrod led them to settle in one place, defying God's design for humanity's expansion.

Let's pause here for a moment. The rebellion at Babel wasn't an isolated event—it was the culmination of humanity's ongoing struggle against divine authority. The seeds of rebellion were planted back in Eden when the serpent sowed doubt in the hearts of Adam and Eve, leading them to seek independence from God. Nimrod's actions echoed that same desire for autonomy, that same temptation to assert human strength and wisdom over God's divine order. It's a recurring theme in the human story, isn't it? How often do we find ourselves trying to build something grand in our own lives, striving for success and independence, while forgetting to seek God's guidance?

The Tower of Babel was much more than just an impressive architectural feat. It was a monument to human pride and rebellion, a symbol of humanity's attempt to control its own destiny. In Genesis 11:4, the people declared, "Come, let us build ourselves a city and a tower with its top in the heavens, and let us make a name for ourselves." Their aim wasn't just to build a tall tower—it was to elevate themselves to godlike status. They sought to reach the heavens on their own terms, independent of God's rule. This ambition mirrors Lucifer's prideful desire to ascend above the heavens and be like the Most High (Isaiah 14:13-14), a pattern of rebellion that continues to resonate in our hearts today.

The Ziggurat Etemenanki: Babel as a Gateway to the Gods

As we explore the significance of Babel, it's essential to recognize its connection to the historical and spiritual symbol of the ziggurat Etemenanki in Babylon. This towering structure, uncovered by archaeologists, reveals the human desire to physically and spiritually bridge the gap between heaven and earth. Etemenanki, meaning "temple of the foundation of heaven and earth," was a massive ziggurat that dominated ancient Babylon's landscape. It wasn't just a place of worship—it symbolized humanity's ambition to directly access the divine, to control that connection on their terms.

Picture the scene: a grand structure rising toward the heavens, built to invoke the presence of the gods. Ziggurats like Etemenanki were designed as stairways between the human and divine realms—literal gateways through which gods were believed to descend to interact with humanity. But the people of Babel weren't seeking the true God. Instead, they wanted to invoke lesser, rebellious spiritual beings—false gods—believing they could control divine power and bend it to their will.

This desire to control the divine lies at the heart of Babel's rebellion. The people weren't just building a tower—they were attempting to bypass God's authority and establish their own path to heaven. This mirrors the rebellion of the fallen angels we discussed in earlier chapters, who sought to transcend their divine roles. In a similar way, Babel's builders wanted to claim divinity for themselves. It's a dangerous pattern that has repeated throughout history: humanity's constant striving to seize control of things meant to be in God's hands.

Reflecting on this, we can't help but notice how Babel's ambition foreshadows the idolatry and spiritual rebellion that would spread across the nations after the scattering. The human heart has a natural inclination to seek power, control, and meaning in the wrong places—an inclination that Babel epitomizes.

The Judgment of Babel: Scattering and Spiritual Disinheritance

God's response to the rebellion at Babel was swift and decisive. He saw the unity of the people, but He also saw the pride and rebellion that fueled their efforts. In Genesis 11:6, God said, "Behold, they are one people, and they all have one language, and this is only the beginning of what they will do. And nothing that they propose to do will now be impossible for them." The issue wasn't just their unity—it was the purpose for which they were unified. If their rebellion went unchecked, it would have led to even greater moral and spiritual decay.

In an act of both judgment and mercy, God confused their language and scattered them across the earth. Imagine the chaos that followed: people who had been working in perfect harmony were suddenly unable to understand one another. The project was abandoned, and the once-unified people were divided into different languages, cultures, and locations. But this scattering was more than just a geographic relocation—it marked a moment of profound spiritual disinheritance.

Deuteronomy 32:8-9 offers us a glimpse into the spiritual dimension of this event: "When the Most High gave to the nations their inheritance, when He divided mankind, He fixed the borders of the peoples according to the number of the sons of God. But the Lord's portion is His people, Jacob His allotted heritage." In this moment, God handed over the rebellious nations to fallen spiritual beings—the "sons of God" who had already turned away from Him. These spiritual beings became the rulers over the nations, leading humanity deeper into idolatry, false worship, and moral corruption.

Consider the gravity of that moment. God essentially said to humanity, "If you want to live apart from Me, I will allow you to experience life under the rule of these fallen beings." The nations were handed over to rebellious spiritual rulers who had no intention of leading them back to God. The result was a world steeped in idolatry, violence, and moral decay.

God's Redemptive Plan Through Israel

The Tower of Babel, once a symbol of human pride, became the backdrop for the unfolding of God's redemptive plan. As the nations scattered, God chose one man, Abraham, to be the father of a people through whom the world would be blessed. The scattering at Babel wasn't the end of the story—it was the beginning of God's plan to reconcile the nations back to Himself.

Deuteronomy 32:8-9 gives us insight into the spiritual dimension of this scattering: "When the Most High gave to the nations their inheritance, when He divided mankind, He fixed the borders of the peoples according to the number of the sons of God. But the Lord's portion is His people, Jacob His allotted heritage". In the scattering, God allowed the nations to follow after rebellious spiritual beings. But from Abraham, God began to reclaim His people.

Through Abram's descendants, God would establish His covenant, a promise that would lead to the arrival of the Messiah. This was the beginning of the redemptive journey—a journey that continues through Christ, who came to gather the nations once again.

Throughout the pages of Section 2: Rebellion, we have traced the origins of disobedience— from the fall in Eden to the grave rebellion of the Sons of God in Genesis 6, and finally, to the defiance at Babel.

We've explored how pride, ambition, and a desire for autonomy fractured the relationship between God and humanity, culminating in the scattering of nations. Yet, even as humanity rebelled, God's mercy and faithfulness never wavered. His intervention at Babel was not the end, but the first step toward restoring what had been broken.

Now, as we move forward into Section 3: Restoration, we will shift our focus from rebellion to redemption. We've laid the foundation for understanding humanity's disobedience, and now we will see how God's plan to heal that fracture unfolds—beginning with the call of Abraham and culminating in the ultimate restoration through Christ. The rebellion of the nations scattered them far from God, but His covenant with Israel would pave the way for all nations to be reconciled and restored.

Origins of Disobedience

Ephesians 6:12

For our struggle is not against flesh and blood, but against the rulers, against the authorities, against the powers of this dark world and against the spiritual forces of evil in the heavenly realms.

Introduction to Section 3 / "Restoration"

As we enter this final section of the book, let's take a moment to reflect on the incredible journey we've been on together. We began by uncovering God's original vision—a breathtaking design of perfect harmony between His spiritual and human families. Picture it: a seamless fellowship between the Divine Council in the heavens and humanity on earth, both reflecting God's glory in moral and relational unity. It's a vision we all long for—a world where everything is as it should be.

But as we journeyed deeper into the story, we witnessed how sin, idolatry, and corruption shattered that harmony. From the fall in Eden to the rebellion at Babel, humanity's pride repeatedly led them away from God. The world fractured, and God's creation was left in desperate need of restoration. Yet even as humanity scattered at Babel, we began to see God's redemptive plan take shape.

God's response to rebellion wasn't to abandon the world, but to set in motion a journey of restoration that would span generations. This journey will begin with the call of Abraham—a man through whom God would build a nation, Israel, and through that nation, bless all the families of the earth. The call of Abraham wasn't just a historical moment; it was the start of God's long-term plan to heal the brokenness of creation and reconcile the nations to Himself.

Now, as we move into Section 3, we're not just recounting history—we're stepping into the heart of God's unfolding plan. This section will be our shared journey through the pages of Scripture, following how God's plan for restoration unfolds. Together, we'll travel alongside the key figures of this story—the main characters God uses to move His redemptive mission forward. From Abraham to Isaac, from Jacob to Moses, from David to the prophets, we'll see how God's faithfulness is passed down through generations, bringing us ever closer to the fulfillment of His promises in Christ.

The call of Abraham marks the beginning of this redemptive journey—a journey we will follow through the lives of the patriarchs and the nation of Israel. Imagine the ripple effect of one man's faith: God's promise to bless all nations through Abraham didn't just shape his life, but laid the foundation for every generation that followed. As we explore this pivotal moment, I encourage you to reflect on your own faith journey. Just as Abraham's call had global implications, so too does your relationship with God. You are part of that same promise, part of the blessing that extends across time and space, touching lives in ways you may not even realize.

As we continue this journey, you'll witness how God's promises take root and grow through wilderness seasons, covenants, and the establishment of a people chosen to reflect His holiness to the world. We'll trace the longing for a righteous King, a King who would ultimately be revealed in Jesus Christ, the true fulfillment of all God's promises. Each of these characters—Abraham, Isaac, Jacob, Moses, David, and others—play crucial roles in God's story of restoration, helping to move His plan forward.

Together, we'll see how the scattered nations of Babel are being drawn back into unity through the life, death, and resurrection of Jesus. The key figures we meet along the way aren't just distant characters of the past—they are threads in a tapestry of restoration that leads to Christ. And His story is our story. The restoration Jesus brings is the fulfillment of everything we've been waiting for, not just for Israel, but for all of creation.

As we explore the Scriptures in this section, remember that this story isn't just about the past. You, dear reader, are part of God's ongoing work of restoration. His plan continues today, drawing you into His eternal mission of redemption.

Chapter 18 – Abraham's Covenant: The Beginning of God's Restoration Plan

As we enter this next chapter, remember that this is not just a historical recounting—it's the foundation of the promises that shape your life today. We've already explored how God's plan of restoration unfolds through key figures like Abraham, Moses, and David. Now, we turn our focus to the beginning of that journey: the call of Abraham and the covenant God made with him. This was no ordinary event. It marked the moment when God's plan to restore a broken world began to take shape—a plan that includes you.

The Call of Abraham: A Personal Shift in Divine Strategy

Imagine a world steeped in idolatry, where people had given themselves over to false gods and corrupt spiritual forces. In that darkness, God called one man—Abraham, then known as Abram—out of a city devoted to the worship of the moon god Nanna. Ur was Abraham's home, a place where people sought guidance from anything but the one true God. Can you picture it? It was in the middle of this spiritual confusion that God's voice broke through, calling Abraham into something completely new.

Genesis 12 tells us how God instructed Abraham to leave behind everything familiar—his country, his people, even his father's household—and journey to a land that He would show him. But this wasn't just about physical distance; it was a spiritual moment of transformation. God was calling Abraham out of idolatry and into a life of faith. This wasn't a small, private decision either. It was the beginning of something much bigger—a reversal of the disinheritance at Babel. While the nations had been scattered and handed over to rebellious spiritual beings, God chose one man to begin His work of restoration.

Can you see how personal this was for Abraham? It wasn't just about leaving home. It was about stepping into a divine mission, one that would ultimately lead to the redemption of the world. In a sense, Abraham's journey is our journey too—a call to leave behind the spiritual confusion and idols that distract us, and to walk by faith toward God's promise.

The Covenant and the Promise: God's Plan to Reclaim the Nations

When we look at the covenant God made with Abraham in Genesis 15, it's clear that this was no small promise. It wasn't just about Abraham's family; it was about the future of humanity itself. Think of the three key elements of the covenant: the promise of land, descendants as numerous as the stars, and a blessing that would reach all nations. These were not merely personal promises to Abraham—they carried the weight of God's cosmic plan for redemption.

Let's unpack that for a moment. The land promised to Abraham wasn't just a piece of territory; it represented the reestablishment of God's rule on earth. It was a sign that God was reclaiming what had been lost at Babel and in Eden. Abraham's descendants, who would become the nation of Israel, were chosen to be the vessel through which God would bring forth the Messiah—the One who would ultimately reconcile heaven and earth. Through this covenant, God was making His first move in a cosmic battle against the forces of darkness that had gripped the world.

Can you feel the weight of that promise? This covenant with Abraham was the foundation for everything that would follow. It was the start of God's mission to restore humanity, not just through Israel but through the Messiah who would come from Abraham's lineage. And the beauty of it is that this covenant extends to you as well. When you place your faith in Christ, you are grafted into that promise, becoming part of God's great plan of reconciliation.

Abraham's Role: Father of Faith, Foundation of Restoration

Abraham's story is often seen as a story of family, but it's so much more. The apostle Paul explains that Abraham's faith became the model for both Jews and Gentiles, the foundation for how we are meant to relate to God. His faith was not based on his own strength or works, but on trusting God's promises, no matter how impossible they seemed. Isn't that something we all wrestle with at times—trusting God when the road ahead looks unclear?

What's remarkable is how Abraham's story shows us that restoration, whether in our personal lives or on a cosmic scale, comes through faith in God's power to redeem, not in our own abilities. Paul even writes that if you belong to Christ, you are Abraham's offspring and heirs according to the promise. This means that the covenant made with Abraham isn't just a promise locked in ancient history—it's alive in your own faith journey today.

When you trust in Christ, you're walking in the same faith that Abraham did, becoming a part of the family God is gathering from every nation. This is the beauty of God's plan: it's not about one ethnicity or one nation, but about bringing all people back into His family through faith. It's a promise that extends to you, inviting you into a relationship with the God who is reclaiming what was lost.

Reconciliation Through Christ: The Fulfillment of the Promise

While Abraham's story marks the beginning, the ultimate fulfillment of the promise comes through Jesus Christ. In Genesis 22, God tells Abraham, "Through your offspring all nations on earth will be blessed." That offspring is Christ—the One who would reconcile not only Israel but all nations to God. Through Jesus' life, death, and resurrection, the power of sin and spiritual darkness that had enslaved humanity was broken.

The apostle Paul reminds us that in Christ, those who were once far off have been brought near through His sacrifice. Jesus is our peace, breaking down the barriers that divide us from God and from one another. The reconciliation Jesus brings is both vertical—between us and God—and horizontal—between us and others. It's through Jesus that the scattered nations, once disinherited, are invited back into a relationship with the living God.

And that includes you. Through Christ, you're not only saved from sin; you are part of God's ongoing work of restoration. The promise made to Abraham reaches its fulfillment in Jesus, and through faith, you share in that blessing.

The Renewal of Creation: A Future Restored

Abraham's story doesn't just look backward; it points us forward to the future restoration God has promised. The covenant with Abraham was the beginning, but Scripture gives us a glimpse of the end—when heaven and earth will be made new, and God will dwell with His people forever. The nations, once scattered and divided, will be gathered together, worshiping the one true God in perfect unity.

This is the ultimate fulfillment of God's promise to Abraham: a future where all things are made new, where the brokenness of sin is forever undone, and where God's family—both heavenly and earthly—live together in harmony. It's a future you are invited into, one that gives meaning and hope to your faith today.

Abraham's Legacy and Your Role

Abraham's journey wasn't just about him, and it's not just a story from the distant past. His faith journey is a living legacy that shapes your life today. The covenant God made with Abraham was the first step in His grand plan to restore humanity, and through faith in Christ, you are part of that promise.

Like Abraham, you are called out of the idols and distractions of this world, whether they take the form of success, materialism, or even self-interest. Just as Abraham was called to leave behind the idolatry of Ur, you are called to leave behind anything that pulls you away from God's purpose. And that purpose is not just about personal growth—it's about being part of God's mission to reconcile the world to Himself.

In the upcoming chapters, we'll take a closer look at The Great Commission, where Jesus tells His followers to go and make disciples of all nations. This is our direct continuation of the promise God made to Abraham. You are called to be a blessing to others, to carry the message of reconciliation to a world that desperately needs it.

So, as you walk in faith, know that you are not just a recipient of God's grace; you are a participant in His mission. Abraham's story is a reminder that God's promises are sure, and His plan is unfolding—even in your life. Just as Abraham looked forward in faith to the fulfillment of God's plan, you too can live with the hope and assurance that one day, all things will be made new. And in that glorious future, the promise made to Abraham will come to its ultimate fulfillment—one that includes you, shaping your faith and your future in Christ.

But Abraham's story of faith and promise was just the beginning. The covenant God made with him was passed down through his descendants, continuing to unfold through his son Isaac and his grandson Jacob. Their lives played pivotal roles in carrying forward the legacy of promise and laying the foundation for the nation of Israel. In the next chapter, we will explore how Isaac and Jacob, despite their struggles and uncertainties, became key figures in God's plan for restoration. Their stories show us how God's faithfulness endures through generations, moving His divine mission closer to fulfillment.

Genesis 12: 1-3

Now the Lord said to Abram, "Go from your country and your kindred and your father's house to the land that I will show you. And I will make of you a great nation, and I will bless you and make your name great, so that you will be a blessing. I will bless those who bless you, and him who dishonors you I will curse, and in you all the families of the earth shall be blessed."

Chapter 19 - The Legacy of Promise: Isaac and Jacob

As we journey through the stories of Isaac and Jacob, remember that these are not merely ancient tales or distant memories. They are living threads woven into the grand tapestry of God's redemptive plan—a plan that began with creation, was rekindled through the call of Abraham, and now continues through his descendants. Isaac and Jacob were not just the next names in a genealogy; they were chosen to carry forward the covenant, entrusted with the continuation of God's promise to restore creation. If we look closely, we can see ourselves in their stories. Their lives are not relics of the past but part of the divine mission that continues today. Through Isaac and Jacob, we witness the unfolding promise of reconciliation and redemption—a promise that, by God's grace, includes us all.

Isaac: The Child of Covenant Promise

Isaac's story is a miracle wrapped in the fabric of divine faithfulness. Imagine waiting your entire life for something that seems impossible. Abraham and Sarah had grown old, far beyond the natural age for children, and yet God had promised them a son. Then, against all odds, Isaac was born—a tangible reminder that God's promises never fail, no matter how impossible they may seem.

Isaac's birth was not just the continuation of Abraham's family line; it was the continuation of the covenant. This covenant wasn't merely a contract or an agreement—it was a divine promise that extended far beyond Abraham's household. It was a promise of blessings that would reach all nations, a promise that God would work through Abraham's descendants to restore what had been broken in creation. Every time we hear Isaac's name, we are reminded that God's word stands firm, no matter the circumstances.

Isaac's life may seem quieter and less dramatic than Abraham's or Jacob's, but his story is a testament to the kind of steady, faithful endurance that often goes unnoticed. Isaac's faithfulness in trusting God, despite moments of passivity, shows us that God's covenant is not dependent on human action but on divine faithfulness. Even in moments of silence, Isaac's life carried forward the promise of God's blessing to the nations.

But Isaac's significance doesn't end with his birth. There's another moment in his life that points to something even deeper—the moment when Abraham, in obedience, prepared to offer his son as a sacrifice on Mount Moriah. This story is hard to grasp, isn't it? The idea of a father being asked to give up his only son is almost too painful to imagine. And yet, here, we see a powerful foreshadowing of the ultimate sacrifice that would take place many generations later. Where Isaac was spared and a ram took his place, Jesus would one day become the Lamb who takes away the sins of the world.

Isaac's near-sacrifice isn't just a historical event; it's a signpost pointing us to Christ. It reminds us that the journey of redemption involves both sacrifice and substitution—themes that we will encounter again and again as we continue through Scripture. Isaac's life may seem quiet compared to the more dramatic stories we've encountered, but it is rich with meaning. He is the quiet bridge, the steady link in a chain that carries God's promises forward, generation by generation.

Jacob: Wrestling with Destiny and Identity

If Isaac's story is one of quiet faithfulness, Jacob's is one of struggle. Can you relate to that? Jacob's life feels so much more human—filled with tension, conflict, and even deceit. From the moment he was born, grasping his twin brother Esau's heel, Jacob's life was marked by a desire for blessing, for position, for more.

It's easy to judge Jacob for his trickery—stealing his brother's birthright and deceiving his father, Isaac. But if we look a little closer, we see something of ourselves in him. How often do we grasp for things, trying to secure our future or our blessings by our own means, instead of trusting God's timing? Jacob's story reminds us that even in our messiest moments, God is still working.

The turning point in Jacob's life comes when he finds himself alone, on the run, wrestling with God. Can you imagine wrestling with God all night? This isn't just a physical struggle; it's a spiritual one. Jacob, who had spent his life trying to manipulate and control his circumstances, is finally forced to confront the deeper questions of identity and purpose. It's in this moment, at Peniel, that everything changes. Jacob is no longer the deceiver. God gives him a new name: Israel, meaning "he who struggles with God." And isn't that what faith sometimes feels like? A struggle. A wrestling match between our desires and God's will. But in the end, we, like Jacob, are transformed by the encounter.

Jacob's struggle with God wasn't just about physical survival—it was a moment of spiritual reckoning. In that long, painful night of wrestling, Jacob confronted his deepest fears, his identity, and the brokenness of his past. It's in this vulnerable, raw encounter that Jacob is transformed, emerging not just with a new name, Israel, but with a new understanding of God's grace. This powerful moment reminds us that true transformation often comes through our most painful struggles—when we stop fighting for control and surrender to God's purpose.

Jacob's life, filled with flaws and failures, is a story of grace. Through him, God's promises continue, not because Jacob is perfect, but because God is faithful. And it's this faithfulness that we see carrying forward as Jacob becomes the father of twelve sons—sons who will become the twelve tribes of Israel.

The Twelve Sons: Seeds of a Nation

Jacob's sons represent so much more than just names in a genealogy; they are the seeds of a nation, the initial sparks of a divine movement destined to shape the future of God's people. Through these twelve tribes, the covenant promise expands from individuals into a national narrative, setting apart a people uniquely chosen for God's purposes. This intricate tapestry weaves together the past, present, and future of redemption.

Picture yourself in the ancient lands where these stories unfold. The air is thick with the scent of livestock, and laughter echoes from nearby tents. This is not just a family gathering; it marks the birth of a nation. Each of Jacob's sons emerges as a distinct thread in the fabric of Israel, carrying the weight of destiny and divine promise. Their stories are rich with lessons that resonate with us today.

Judah: The Line of Promise

Among these sons, Judah stands out as a forerunner of something monumental. From his lineage will spring forth the kings of Israel, culminating in the King of Kings—Jesus Christ. This legacy begins with a man who was, at times, far from perfect. Judah's life reflects God's grace and mercy, showing that He can use flawed individuals to accomplish His divine plans.

Imagine Jacob blessing his sons, speaking words of prophecy and significance over each of them. In a world that often overlooks individual value, we see God affirming the unique roles each son will play. Judah's selection to carry the royal line serves as a testament to God's ability to see beyond human failures. This truth is profoundly comforting: God's plans are not contingent on our perfection but are rooted in His unchanging nature and purpose.

The Broader Picture: Twelve Tribes, One Mission

As we explore the lives of the other eleven sons—Reuben, Simeon, Levi, Dan, Naphtali, Gad, Asher, Issachar, Zebulun, Joseph, and Benjamin—we discover a mosaic of experiences that contribute to the identity of Israel. Each son brings forth unique characteristics and stories, reflecting various facets of the human experience, from conflict and rivalry to loyalty and love. Their interactions and struggles remind us that God's people are not immune to strife; they grow through it, learning to lean on His grace.

Consider Joseph, who endures betrayal and hardship yet rises to prominence in Egypt, ultimately saving his family from famine. His journey teaches us about resilience and forgiveness, embodying the spirit of redemption that God seeks to cultivate. The foundation of Israel is built not just on triumphs but also on trials, each moment meticulously crafted to prepare them for their divine mission.

A Nation Set Apart: The Hope of the World

Together, these twelve tribes form a nation destined to embody God's covenant promises. Their identity is not rooted solely in heritage but in purpose. They are called to reflect God's glory, be a light to the nations, and bear witness to His redemptive power. Their story intertwines with ours, prompting us to consider our role in the ongoing narrative of God's kingdom.

As we reflect on Jacob's sons, we recognize that we are part of a larger story that transcends time and place. Just as each tribe contributed to the unfolding of God's plan, our lives play a part in His redemptive work today. Though we may not descend from Judah, as followers of Christ, we are adopted into this family, inheriting the promises and responsibilities that come with it.

Imperfect People, Unchanging God

Reflecting on Isaac and Jacob, one truth emerges: God's plan doesn't depend on perfect people. Isaac was passive, while Jacob was a deceiver striving to get ahead. Yet, God's promises advance. This is comforting; God's faithfulness is the constant in a world filled with human weakness. He works through flawed individuals to fulfill His purposes. Isaac and Jacob remind us that God's covenant isn't about human merit but divine grace.

Generation after generation, God moves His plan of restoration forward. What began with Abraham continues through Isaac and Jacob and will ultimately find fulfillment in Christ. Their stories not only continue God's promises but also mark the beginning of a nation through whom the world will be blessed.

Looking Ahead: From Family to Nation

As we turn the page to the next chapter, we will witness Jacob's twelve sons become the twelve tribes of Israel. This narrative shifts from a family to a nation, exploring how Israel will bear the weight of God's covenant promises.

The journey won't be easy. Like Isaac and Jacob, Israel's story will feature moments of faith and failure. Yet, God's unshakable faithfulness remains the central theme. The nation of Israel, born from Jacob's lineage, will pave the way for the ultimate redemption through Christ.

The lives of Isaac and Jacob are more than historical accounts; they are threads in the grand tapestry of God's plan to restore what was lost in Eden. Through their faith, struggles, and failures, we see a God who never abandons His creation. He is a God who works through imperfect people, weaving together a redemptive story that leads us to Christ, the fulfillment of all the covenant promises.

Genesis 35: 10-11

And God said to him, "Your name is Jacob; no longer shall your name be called Jacob, but Israel shall be your name." So, he called his name Israel. And God said to him, "I am God Almighty: be fruitful and multiply. A nation and a company of nations shall come from you, and kings shall come from your own body.

Exodus 19: 18-20

Now Mount Sinai was wrapped in smoke because the Lord had descended on it in fire. The smoke of it went up like the smoke of a kiln, and the whole mountain trembled greatly. And as the sound of the trumpet grew louder and louder, Moses spoke, and God answered him in thunder. The Lord came down on Mount Sinai, to the top of the mountain. And the Lord called Moses to the top of the mountain, and Moses went up..

Chapter 20 - Establishing a Holy Nation
Covenants and Commandments

As we leave behind the personal stories of Isaac, Jacob, and their sons, we now turn to the next chapter in the unfolding story of God's covenant. What began as promises to a family now expands to shape an entire people. The twelve tribes of Israel, descendants of Jacob's sons, are about to experience a transformation unlike any before—their journey from slavery to freedom, from a family to a nation set apart by God.

The story of the Exodus is not just a historical account of liberation; it is a pivotal moment in God's divine narrative—a turning point where His plan for humanity takes shape in ways that still resonate today. Imagine the weight of this moment as you reflect on Israel's journey from slavery to becoming a holy nation, uniquely chosen to embody God's covenant promises. This moment is a beacon of hope, not just for Israel but for all nations, as it illuminates God's redemptive design.

Every detail of the Exodus—from God's divine calling of Moses to the monumental giving of the Law at Mount Sinai—shapes the identity and destiny of Israel. As you consider the gravity of these events, you might sense God's unwavering faithfulness in delivering His people from oppression. This is more than just history; it's a profound testament to God's relentless love and commitment, reminding us that His promises endure through generations.

The Call of Moses: A Divine Commission

The Exodus story begins in the wilderness, where Moses, once a prince of Egypt, now tends sheep in Midian after fleeing from his past. He is living in obscurity, disconnected from his people. Yet, in this remote and ordinary place, something extraordinary happens. In Exodus 3,

Moses witnesses a bush ablaze with fire but not consumed. God speaks to him from within the flames:

"I have surely seen the affliction of My people who are in Egypt and have heard their cry because of their taskmasters. I know their sufferings, and I have come down to deliver them out of the hand of the Egyptians." (Exodus 3:7-8)

In this divine encounter, Moses transitions from fugitive to divinely appointed leader. God calls him to return to Egypt, not as the man who fled, but as a messenger of liberation. Like Moses, we often feel unqualified or distant from God's purpose, but it is precisely in these moments that God invites us into something extraordinary. How might God be calling you, even in your ordinary circumstances, to step into His extraordinary plans?

God's words to Moses reveal His deep concern for His people's suffering and His unwavering commitment to His covenant promises. The burning bush, an image of God's holiness, reminds us that God is self-sustaining and all-powerful. Just as the fire did not consume the bush, God's covenant promises remain unbroken and unshaken, even through the most difficult circumstances.

The Plagues: Demonstrating God's Power

Pharaoh's heart hardens, and his refusal to release the Israelites sets in motion a series of ten plagues, each a direct challenge to the Egyptian gods. Imagine the growing tension as these divine acts unfold—a powerful display of God's authority over creation and His desire to make His name known, not just to Israel, but to the nations.

The first plague, the turning of the Nile to blood, confronts Hapi, the Egyptian god of the Nile, asserting Yahweh's dominion over the very source of life in Egypt. Each plague that follows—frogs, gnats, flies, livestock disease—targets specific Egyptian deities. Frogs, sacred to fertility gods, become a curse. Livestock, revered by the Egyptians, are struck with disease. Through each plague, Yahweh systematically dismantles the power of Egypt's gods, demonstrating that He alone is sovereign.

In Exodus 7:5, God declares, "The Egyptians shall know that I am the Lord when I stretch out My hand against Egypt and bring out the people of Israel from among them." Each plague is more than a judgment—it's a divine proclamation of God's power over all false gods. When the final plague takes the lives of the Egyptian firstborn, even Pharaoh cannot stand against Yahweh. This climactic moment dismantles the Egyptian religious system, clarifying for both Israel and future generations that Yahweh is sovereign over all creation.

The plagues are not mere acts of punishment; they are demonstrations of God's unyielding commitment to His people. They reveal His desire to free Israel and establish them as a holy nation. The journey from slavery to freedom is being orchestrated step by step, preparing them for the Law they will receive at Mount Sinai.

The Passover: A Sacrifice of Protection

As the final plague approaches, bringing the death of the firstborn in every Egyptian household, God provides a way of escape for His people. In Exodus 12, He instructs the Israelites to sacrifice a lamb and mark their doorposts with its blood. This blood becomes a sign for the Lord to pass over their homes, sparing them from the final judgment:

"The blood shall be a sign for you, on the houses where you are. And when I see the blood, I will pass over you, and no plague will befall you to destroy you, when I strike the land of Egypt."(Exodus 12:13)

This moment is not only crucial for the immediate deliverance of Israel, but it also foreshadows the ultimate sacrifice of Jesus Christ, the Lamb of God. Just as the blood on the doorposts protected Israel from death, Christ's blood shields us from the eternal consequences of sin. The Passover is more than a moment of deliverance; it is a picture of redemption that points directly to the cross. Through His sacrifice, Jesus delivers us from spiritual death and offers us eternal life.

For Israel, the Passover became an annual reminder of God's faithfulness, and for us, it symbolizes the ultimate deliverance through Christ. It's a reminder that God's plan for salvation has been unfolding since the very beginning, always pointing to Jesus.

The Crossing of the Red Sea: A New Identity

After the tenth plague, Pharaoh finally releases the Israelites. Yet, as they approach the Red Sea, they find themselves trapped—Pharaoh has changed his mind and is now pursuing them with his army. With the sea in front of them and their enemies closing in, the situation seems hopeless. But God instructs Moses to raise his staff over the waters. As he obeys, the sea parts, allowing the Israelites to cross on dry ground.

This act of salvation signifies far more than just physical deliverance. It marks a profound transformation in Israel's identity. No longer slaves, they emerge as a redeemed nation, set apart for God's divine purposes. In stepping through the parted sea, they leave behind their bondage and fully embrace the new life God has prepared for them.

This moment beautifully foreshadows the Christian experience of baptism, where believers leave behind their old lives of sin and step into new life in Christ. Just as the Israelites entered the waters of the Red Sea as slaves and emerged as a free people, we are invited to recognize our identity as new creations in Christ, marked by God's grace and love.

The Giving of the Law: A Framework for Holiness

As the Israelites journey through the wilderness, they come to Mount Sinai, where they will experience a momentous event, the giving of the

Law. This is not just a pivotal moment in Israel's story, but also a key moment in the unfolding of God's redemptive plan for humanity. Here, God establishes a divine blueprint for how His people are to live in covenant relationship with Him.

In Exodus 19:5-6, God declares, "Now therefore, if you will indeed obey My voice and keep My covenant, you shall be My treasured possession among all peoples." The Law is more than a set of rules—it is an invitation to live in close relationship with God. He desires His people to reflect His holiness, justice, and love to the nations. The Law reveals God's heart for His people, calling them to walk in His ways and to know Him more deeply.

Each commandment is designed to foster a community rooted in justice, mercy, and righteousness. The Law helps Israel understand what it means to be God's chosen people, set apart to reflect His character. But it's not just about individual behavior—it's about building a society that embodies God's compassion and justice. The Law calls Israel to care for the marginalized, to pursue honesty and integrity, and to love one another as God loves them.

The giving of the Law at Sinai is a transformative moment, shaping Israel's identity as a people chosen for a purpose. It's an invitation into a life of holiness, not just for Israel, but for all who follow God. Through the Law, God reveals His commitment to His people and calls them to reflect His character in a world desperately in need of His light.

Reflection: Our Journey of Faith

As we consider these foundational events of the Exodus, we are invited to reflect on our own journeys of faith. Just as God delivered Israel from physical bondage, He delivers us from spiritual bondage through Jesus Christ. The blood of the Passover lamb foreshadows the blood of Christ, which covers and protects us from the ultimate consequence of sin—spiritual death.

Where are you in your journey of faith? Perhaps you feel trapped by your circumstances, facing obstacles as daunting as the Red Sea. Or maybe you're waiting for God's deliverance, unsure of how He will make a way. Like Israel, we are called to trust that God will part the waters in our lives, even when the path forward seems impossible.

Just as the Israelites emerged from the Red Sea as a new people, we, too, are called to embrace our identity in Christ. The Law given to Israel at Sinai serves as a reminder that God desires a close, intimate relationship with His people. He calls us not just to follow rules, but to live in a way that reflects His love and justice in the world.

As you reflect on the Exodus, consider how God is working in your own life. He is still writing His story of redemption, and you are part of that story. Whether you are in a season of waiting, crossing through a difficult sea, or receiving new revelation, God is leading you forward. He is calling you to trust in His promises, to walk in His ways, and to be a light to the world around you.

Chapter 21 - Conquering Canaan: A Divine Promise Fulfilled

As we move from the powerful events at Mount Sinai, where God gave His people the Law, we now enter a new and decisive phase in Israel's journey—a journey that would test their faith, challenge their courage, and shape their identity as a nation. The Law had established Israel as a holy people, but the true test of their faithfulness lay ahead. The wilderness would test their trust in God, and the Promised Land would challenge their ability to confront both physical and spiritual obstacles. This journey, from the wilderness to Canaan, was more than a change in geography; it was a movement from slavery to freedom, from wandering to purpose, and from fear to faith.

The Wilderness: A Testing Ground of Faith

After their dramatic deliverance from Egypt and the covenant established at Mount Sinai, the Israelites entered into a long and difficult season of wandering in the wilderness. At first glance, this 40-year period may seem like punishment for their disobedience, but it was also a time of preparation. The wilderness became a divine classroom, where God shaped His people, tested their hearts, and taught them to rely on Him for every need. It wasn't merely a journey of survival—it was a journey of transformation.

Moses reflects on this in Deuteronomy 8:2:

"And you shall remember the whole way that the Lord your God has led you these forty years in the wilderness, that He might humble you, testing you to know what was in your heart, whether you would keep His commandments or not."

The wilderness was a place where Israel learned what it meant to trust God completely, even in the midst of uncertainty. Yet, it was also a place where their weaknesses and doubts were revealed. Despite God's continual provision—sending manna from heaven, water from rocks, and guiding them with a cloud by day and fire by night—the people often grumbled and longed for the comforts of Egypt (Exodus 16:3). Their faith wavered time and again.

The most significant failure of faith occurred at Kadesh Barnea, where Moses sent twelve spies to scout the Promised Land. Upon returning, ten of the spies gave a fearful report, highlighting the presence of giants—the descendants of the Nephilim—and declaring that Israel would never be able to defeat them (Numbers 13:31-33). Fear spread through the camp like wildfire, and the people, paralyzed by doubt, rebelled against God.

Imagine standing on the brink of God's promises, only to turn away because fear seemed more real than faith. How often do we face similar moments, where fear causes us to hesitate or retreat from what God has called us to?

In contrast, Joshua and Caleb urged the people to trust in God's power, confident that He would deliver the land into their hands. But the majority refused to believe, and the consequence was severe: an entire generation was sentenced to die in the wilderness, never to see the land promised to their ancestors (Numbers 14:26-35). Still, God's mercy remained. Even in their rebellion, He continued to provide food, water, and guidance, preparing a new generation to enter the land.

The Battle Against the Giants: Confronting the Nephilim Legacy

Before Israel could inherit the Promised Land, they had to confront a formidable and mysterious enemy: the Nephilim. The Bible first introduces the Nephilim in Genesis 6:4, describing them as the offspring of the "sons of God" and human women, renowned for their great size and strength. Although the flood wiped them out, Scripture indicates that they somehow reappeared in Canaan. The Anakim, descendants of the Nephilim, were the giants that terrified the ten spies.

The Nephilim represented more than just a physical threat. They embodied a spiritual legacy of rebellion, a defiance against God that had persisted since the earliest days of humanity. The battle against the Nephilim wasn't just a military confrontation; it was a spiritual struggle, a battle to reclaim the land for God's purposes.

In many ways, the Nephilim symbolize the challenges we face in our own lives. Just as the Israelites had to confront these giants, we too must confront the "giants" that threaten to overwhelm us—giants of fear, doubt, sin, and insecurity. The presence of the Nephilim serves as a reminder that we, like Israel, face spiritual battles in our daily lives, battles that test our faith and resolve.

While the Bible doesn't provide a detailed explanation for how the Nephilim reappeared after the flood, their presence in Canaan signals that Israel's conquest wasn't only about claiming territory—it was about overcoming spiritual strongholds that had long opposed God's redemptive plan.

Overcoming Giants: Faith in the Face of Fear

When the Israelites finally stood at the edge of the Promised Land, they faced both anticipation and fear. The report of the ten spies had stirred terror in their hearts as they described the giants in the land—the Anakim, descendants of the Nephilim. "We seemed to ourselves like grasshoppers," they said, "and so we seemed to them" (Numbers 13:33). The people's fear was paralyzing, leading them to doubt God's ability to deliver on His promise.

But the Nephilim weren't just physical giants; they represented ancient rebellion and defiance against God. The Israelites found themselves at a crossroads, facing not only a physical enemy but a spiritual one as well. It was a moment that demanded faith.

In this critical moment, Joshua's leadership stood out. Unlike the ten spies, Joshua believed in God's promise, trusting that the giants' size was insignificant compared to God's power. When God commissioned Joshua, He gave him this command:

"Be strong and courageous. Do not be frightened, and do not be dismayed, for the Lord your God is with you wherever you go" (Joshua 1:9).

This was more than a call to courage—it was a reminder that the real battle was the Lord's. The conquest of Canaan wasn't about human strength; it was about faith in God's power.

The first victory came at Jericho, where Israel saw the walls of the city fall—not by might, but by obedient faith (Joshua 6:20). This victory set the tone for the entire campaign, showing that the true strength behind Israel's conquest was God Himself.

Later, the Israelites faced the Anakim again, the very giants who had caused them so much fear. But this time, they were no longer paralyzed by doubt. In Joshua 11:21-22, we read that Joshua cut off the Anakim from the hill country, leaving none of the giants in the land. This was not only a military victory but a spiritual triumph over the fear and rebellion that had once gripped the people.

The Conquest of Canaan: Inheriting the Promise

Under Joshua's leadership, the conquest of Canaan became a powerful demonstration of God's faithfulness. Every battle reinforced that it was God who fought for Israel. Joshua 10:42 captures this truth:

"And Joshua captured all these kings and their land at one time, because the Lord God of Israel fought for Israel."

The conquest wasn't just about acquiring land—it was about the fulfillment of God's covenant with Abraham, a promise passed down through Isaac, Jacob, and the twelve tribes of Israel. The land symbolized God's faithfulness and His desire to dwell among His people.

However, the conquest came with a critical warning. God commanded the Israelites to resist the corrupt practices of the Canaanites, whose idolatry had polluted the land. The conquest was both the fulfillment of a promise and a divine judgment against the sin that had taken root in Canaan. Israel was called to be a holy nation, set apart for God's purposes, and the land was to be cleansed of spiritual corruption.

This wasn't just a military campaign—it was a spiritual reclamation of the land for God, a part of the larger struggle between good and evil, and a step toward the ultimate restoration of creation.

As we reflect on Israel's journey from the wilderness to the Promised Land, we see a story of faith, obedience, and the fulfillment of divine promises. The wilderness wasn't merely a time of testing; it was a period of preparation for the spiritual battles that lay ahead. The conquest of Canaan wasn't just about acquiring land—it was about fulfilling God's redemptive plan for His people and the land they were given.

But as Israel settled into the land, they faced new challenges—this time, from within. With Joshua's leadership nearing its end, the nation stood at a crossroads. Who would lead them now? How would they maintain their identity as a people set apart for God?

The transition from conquest to settlement marked the beginning of a new era. Israel would face cycles of disobedience and deliverance, as God raised up Judges to guide and rescue them in times of distress. Yet, these temporary leaders could only do so much. Over time, the people's desire for stability and unity would lead them to cry out for a king—a human ruler like the nations around them.

The period of the Judges was a bridge between Israel's conquest of the land and their transition into a monarchy. It was a time of uncertainty, marked by both divine deliverance and human failure. And soon, Israel would ask for a king, seeking earthly leadership even as God remained their ultimate sovereign.

As we move into the next chapter, we will explore how the period of the Judges laid the foundation for kingship in Israel, and how God continued to weave His plan of restoration through the rise of Israel's monarchy.

Exodus 6:8

I will bring you into the land that I swore to give to Abraham, to Isaac, and to Jacob. I will give it to you for a possession. I am the Lord.

Chapter 22 - A Bridge to Kingship: The Transition from Judges to Monarchy

The period of the Judges marks a pivotal chapter in Israel's story—one defined by cycles of sin, oppression, repentance, and divine deliverance. Through this turbulent era, we witness how the lack of centralized leadership allowed chaos and disobedience to take root, creating a longing for stability and unity among the people. This yearning would eventually lead to the establishment of the monarchy, a significant shift that ultimately points toward God's larger plan for reconciliation, restoration, and redemption. The period of the Judges and the rise of the kings were all part of the divine tapestry woven throughout the Bible, foreshadowing the coming of the true King who would bring lasting peace.

The Need for Leadership

After the death of Joshua, Israel entered a period of instability. Without a strong, unifying leader, the nation drifted into disobedience and idolatry. Judges 2:10-12 paints a tragic picture of this time:

"And all that generation also were gathered to their fathers. And there arose another generation after them who did not know the Lord or the work that He had done for Israel."

Disconnected from the great acts of God that had delivered their ancestors, this new generation strayed from the covenant, opening the door to oppression by surrounding nations. One of the most notable oppressors was the Midianites, whose cruelty brought Israel to the brink of despair (Judges 6:1). When God's people neglect their covenant with Him, chaos inevitably follows.

This pattern is not just an ancient one. How often do we, too, experience cycles of faithfulness and disobedience? Israel's story is a mirror reflecting our own struggles—where neglecting God's guidance leads to personal and communal disorder. The warnings in Deuteronomy 28 about the blessings of obedience and the consequences of disobedience continue to echo in our lives, reminding us that our relationship with God is foundational to every other aspect of life.

The Role of the Judges

In response to Israel's cries for help, God, in His mercy, raised up judges—temporary leaders who would deliver the people from their oppressors and guide them back to covenant faithfulness. Judges 2:16 sums up God's compassion during this period:

"Then the Lord raised up judges, who saved them out of the hand of those who plundered them."

Each judge reflected God's character in different ways, but all of them served as instruments of divine deliverance. For example, Deborah, both a prophetess and a warrior, stood out as a leader who not only called Israel to victory over their enemies but also rekindled their spiritual awareness (Judges 4:6). Her leadership reminds us that God can use anyone—man or woman—to lead in moments of crisis, awakening His people to their covenant responsibilities.

Then there was Gideon, who began as a man of doubt and fear, but was transformed into a courageous leader. With only 300 men, Gideon, by trusting in God's guidance, led Israel to a miraculous victory over the Midianites (Judges 7:7). His story teaches us that God's power is made perfect in our weakness. The victory was a reminder to Israel that their strength came not from numbers or might, but from their reliance on the Lord.

Samson, one of the most complex figures among the judges, was marked by personal failings and tragic choices, yet God still used him to deliver Israel from the Philistines (Judges 13-16). His story reveals that even flawed individuals can be instruments of God's plan, reminding us that our weaknesses do not disqualify us from being used by Him.

Each judge was a temporary solution to Israel's recurring disobedience. While their leadership offered moments of deliverance, it became clear that the nation needed something more—a stable, long-term leadership that could unify the people and guide them in lasting faithfulness.

The Yearning for a King

Despite the deliverance brought by the judges, Israel remained trapped in cycles of sin and oppression. The repeated refrain, "Everyone did what was right in his own eyes" (Judges 21:25), summarizes the spiritual decline and moral chaos that permeated the nation. Without a central leader, the people floundered, seeking stability but failing to maintain it.

In their cry for a king (1 Samuel 8:5), the Israelites weren't just looking for governance—they were searching for identity and unity. The desire for a king, like those of the surrounding nations, reflected a deeper longing for order in the face of fragmentation. However, this request also exposed a profound spiritual problem: the people were seeking human solutions instead of recognizing God as their true King.

Their desire for a king was more than a political move—it was a symptom of their lack of trust in God's leadership. They had forgotten the many times God had delivered them, choosing instead to rely on what they could see—a visible, human ruler—rather than the invisible but all-powerful God. Their request revealed their spiritual insecurity, a longing for control that mirrored their neighbors, rather than resting in their unique identity as God's chosen people.

We, too, face similar struggles. How often do we, like the Israelites, seek human solutions when God calls us to trust in His sovereign leadership? Their request for a king reflects our tendency to rely on earthly powers, material comforts, or even our own understanding rather than fully trusting in God's plan.

The Transition to Monarchy

In His mercy, God did not abandon His people even in their misplaced demands. Instead, He granted their request for a king but used it to further His redemptive plan. He instructed Samuel, the last judge, to anoint Saul as Israel's first king. However, Saul's reign would soon reveal the dangers of leadership disconnected from God's heart. His failure to lead with righteousness and obedience led to his downfall, making way for David—a man chosen not for his outward strength, but for his heart aligned with God's purposes (1 Samuel 16:7).

David's rise to kingship marked a profound turning point in Israel's history. While Saul represented the dangers of human ambition detached from divine guidance, David was a king after God's own heart (Acts 13:22). Though David had personal failings, his reign embodied the hope of godly leadership and set the stage for something greater—a royal line that would eventually lead to the Messiah.

Through David, God established a covenant that promised an eternal dynasty, one that would point to the coming of the ultimate King, Jesus Christ (2 Samuel 7:16). David's reign foreshadowed the coming of a perfect King—one who would rule with righteousness, justice, and mercy. This covenant with David was not just a promise for Israel; it was a promise for all humanity, pointing toward the ultimate restoration that would come through Christ.

God's Use of Judges and Kings

he periods of the Judges and the monarchy were not disconnected events; rather, they were both essential parts of God's grand plan for restoring His people. The judges were temporary deliverers raised up in times of crisis, while the monarchy introduced a more enduring form of leadership through which God's covenant promises would be fully realized.

The judges demonstrated God's mercy and willingness to intervene despite Israel's repeated rebellion. Their leadership, though flawed and temporary, pointed to God's compassion and His desire to restore His people when they cried out for help. But their deliverance was not enough to bring lasting peace, and the cycles of disobedience continued.

The monarchy, particularly through David, laid the foundation for the long-term leadership that Israel needed. It introduced stability and unity, yet the true significance of the monarchy was not in its political or military achievements—it was in its role within God's larger redemptive plan. Through the line of David, God would bring forth the promised Savior, fulfilling His covenant with Abraham to bless all nations through his descendants (Genesis 12:3).

Jesus, the Son of David, would become the ultimate King—the one who would fulfill all the hopes and promises that Israel's judges and kings could only point toward. The judges met immediate needs, offering temporary deliverance, but the monarchy laid the groundwork for the eternal kingship of Christ, the King who would bring about true and lasting restoration.

From Judges to Kings: God's Sovereign Plan

The transition from the judges to the monarchy illustrates God's continual involvement in His people's lives, even when they failed to fully trust Him. The judges were raised up to meet immediate needs, but their leadership was incomplete. Israel needed more than temporary deliverance—they needed a King who would establish an everlasting kingdom, one built on righteousness, justice, and divine faithfulness.

Though Israel's demand for a king arose from insecurity and misplaced trust, God used their request to further His redemptive plan. Saul's failure and David's rise highlighted the flaws in human leadership but also pointed forward to the perfect kingship of Christ. The monarchy ultimately became a stepping stone in God's divine strategy, leading to the arrival of the Messiah, the true King whose reign would bring salvation and restoration to the world.

As we move into the next chapter, we will explore the reign of David, a pivotal moment in Israel's history. David's kingship was not just about ruling a nation; it was about setting the stage for the coming of the true King, Jesus Christ.

1 Samuel 10: 24

And Samuel said to all the people, "Do you see him whom the Lord has chosen? There is none like him among all the people." And all the people shouted, "Long live the king!"

Chapter 23 - The Davidic Covenant: The Promise of an Eternal King

As we continue our journey through the story of Israel, we witness the unfolding of God's redemptive plan, beginning with the call of Abraham, continuing through the Exodus, and the giving of the Law at Mount Sinai. Each pivotal moment reveals more than just a historical event—it unveils God's deep desire to restore His relationship with humanity. From the Garden of Eden, where God walked with Adam and Eve, to the Tabernacle in the wilderness, where His presence dwelled among His people, the theme of God longing to dwell with His creation is ever-present.

Yet, despite these covenantal advancements, the full restoration remained out of reach. The Law provided guidelines for the Israelites to live as God's chosen people, and the Tabernacle served as a reminder of His abiding presence. But something was still missing—a leader who could embody God's rule on earth and unify Israel spiritually and politically under divine sovereignty.

As the Israelites settled into the Promised Land, the limitations of the judge-led system became increasingly evident. The people clamored for a king, yearning for stability, unity, and security against external threats. However, their cry for a monarch revealed a deeper spiritual struggle—the temptation to conform to the surrounding nations instead of trusting God as their true King. Though God granted their request, the reign of their first king, Saul, quickly exposed the perils of leadership disconnected from divine allegiance. Saul's disobedience and tragic failure paved the way for God to raise up a new leader—a king after His own heart.

David: A Heart Aligned with God

David's rise from humble shepherd to the throne of Israel is one of the most remarkable stories in Scripture. Anointed by the prophet Samuel, David's journey was shaped by moments that would prepare him for kingship—none more famous than his victory over Goliath. Yet what truly set David apart was not his military prowess but his deep devotion to God. Unlike Saul, who let his heart stray from the Lord, David sought to align his life with God's will. This exemplifies a core biblical truth: true leadership begins with a heart surrendered to God.

David was not just a king; he was also a poet, a musician, and a man of deep faith. His psalms reveal an intimate relationship with God, expressing praise, worship, and repentance from the depths of his soul. David's authentic love for God demonstrates that spiritual leadership is rooted not in outward success but in a genuine desire to walk closely with the Lord. His reign was shaped by this devotion, and Israel thrived under his leadership because of his heart's alignment with God.

David's Failures and Redemption

However, David's life was far from perfect. His sins and failures serve as reminders of human frailty, and his story is marked by moral failures that had severe consequences—not only for him but for the entire nation. The most infamous of these was his sin with Bathsheba, a moment that led to deceit, adultery, and the murder of her husband, Uriah. David's failure is stark, showing that even a man after God's own heart could succumb to temptation.

But what distinguished David was not the absence of sin, but his response to it. Confronted by the prophet Nathan, David didn't harden his heart or make excuses. Instead, he turned to God in deep repentance, crying out in Psalm 51, "Create in me a clean heart, O God, and renew a right spirit within me." This psalm is a window into

David's soul, showing a man broken by his own sin yet earnestly seeking restoration. David's willingness to confess and repent marked the depth of his relationship with God.

This moment of repentance reveals an important truth: God's plan for redemption is not thwarted by human failure. David's story shows that God's covenant is based not on human perfection but on divine grace. Even in his brokenness, David remained part of God's plan, foreshadowing the need for a greater King—a sinless Messiah—who would bring the ultimate restoration.

The Transformative Reign of David

David's reign was a transformative period for Israel, marked by both political stability and spiritual renewal. One of his most significant acts was establishing Jerusalem as the nation's political and spiritual center. By bringing the Ark of the Covenant into the city, David not only unified Israel but also reaffirmed the nation's calling as a holy people set apart for God. Jerusalem became more than just a political capital; it became a symbol of God's presence among His people, and David's heart was to align the nation with God's will.

Under David's leadership, Israel began to embody its identity as a people governed by divine principles. His psalms, which capture his longing for God's closeness, reflected a vision of justice, mercy, and worship that David sought to instill throughout the nation. David's leadership flourished not just because of his military successes, but because his reign was grounded in his relationship with God.

The Davidic Covenant: Establishing an Eternal Dynasty

In 2 Samuel 7, we encounter one of the most pivotal moments in the biblical narrative: God's covenant with David. After David expressed a desire to build a permanent temple for the Lord, God shifted the focus. Instead of allowing David to construct a house for God, God promised to establish a house for David—an eternal dynasty. This Davidic Covenant carried profound significance and unfolded in three major promises:

A Lasting Dynasty: God assured David that his descendants would form a lasting royal line. This promise went beyond establishing a stable monarchy for Israel; it pointed to an eternal kingdom.

A Chosen Son: God revealed that David's son, Solomon, would build the temple—a permanent dwelling for God's presence among His people. The temple symbolized God's closeness and His desire to dwell with His people.

An Eternal Kingdom: Most significantly, God promised that David's throne would endure forever. This promise extended far beyond the reign of David and Solomon, anticipating the coming of a future King who would reign eternally—a King who would bring lasting peace and restore creation.

The Davidic Covenant became a cornerstone of God's redemptive plan. It was through David's lineage that God would bring forth the Messiah—the eternal King who would reconcile all of creation to Himself. This covenant is more than a historical moment; it is a divine promise pointing to the ultimate restoration that God would accomplish through Jesus Christ.

The Role of the Prophets in Preserving the Promise

As Israel's kings after David fell into cycles of sin and rebellion, the role of the prophets became crucial in preserving the hope of the Davidic Covenant. Prophets like Isaiah, Jeremiah, and Ezekiel called Israel to repentance while continually pointing to the promise of a future King from David's line—a Messiah who would reign with righteousness and justice.

Even in the midst of exile and national despair, the prophets reminded the people that God's covenant with David was still in effect. Isaiah prophesied of a child who would sit on David's throne and establish an eternal kingdom (Isaiah 9:6-7), while Jeremiah spoke of a righteous Branch from David's line (Jeremiah 23:5), who would restore the people and bring peace. These prophetic voices were vital in keeping alive the hope of the promised Messiah, even as Israel faced judgment and exile.

The prophets' messages not only kept Israel's hope alive but also prepared the people for the ultimate fulfillment of the Davidic Covenant in Christ. Their words bridged the gap between Israel's present struggles and the future coming of a righteous King who would reign forever.

The Eternal King: Fulfillment in Christ

The Davidic Covenant finds its ultimate fulfillment in Jesus Christ, often called the Son of David. Jesus is the eternal King promised through David's lineage, who came not only to reconcile Israel to God but to reconcile all nations. The New Testament reveals Jesus as the embodiment of the Davidic Covenant, the King whose reign will never end.

Jesus' kingdom transcends Israel, extending to all nations and all peoples. Through Christ, God's promise to bless all nations through Abraham was realized. His life, death, and resurrection inaugurated the kingdom of God—a kingdom that is already at work in the world and will be fully realized upon His return.

Jesus' kingship is universal. It fulfills not only Israel's hope for a Messiah but extends the promise of the Davidic Covenant to the entire world. The kingdom He established is one that transcends borders and nationalities, welcoming all who call Him Lord into the eternal reign of God.

Connecting the Narrative of Restoration

The Davidic Covenant plays a central role in God's overarching story of restoration. Every pivotal moment in Scripture—from the promise to Abraham, through the Exodus, to the giving of the Law—has pointed toward God's ultimate design to redeem humanity. The promise of an eternal King in David's line is a critical piece of that plan, culminating in Jesus Christ, who fulfills all of God's promises and brings about the reconciliation of all things.

As we prepare for the next chapter, we will explore how Solomon's reign fits into God's redemptive plan. And learn just how Solomon's wisdom and the construction of the temple symbolized Israel's renewed relationship with God.

1 Kings 1:39

There Zadok the priest took the horn of oil from the tent and anointed Solomon.

Chapter 24 - The Road to Restoration: Lessons from Solomon's Reign

The reign of King Solomon stands as one of the most pivotal moments in Israel's history, filled with both triumph and tragedy. Solomon, the son of David, brought Israel into a golden age of wisdom, wealth, and influence. However, his reign also serves as a cautionary tale, highlighting the dangers of spiritual complacency and the consequences of drifting away from God. Through Solomon's story, we are invited to explore profound themes of reconciliation, restoration, and redemption—concepts that permeate the entire biblical narrative and point us toward God's ultimate plan for humanity. As we journey through Solomon's reign, we'll examine how his wisdom, the construction of the Temple, his prosperity, and eventual spiritual decline reveal essential lessons about our relationship with God.

The Gift of Wisdom: A Divine Beginning

Solomon's reign begins not with military conquest or political ambition, but with a dream—a divine encounter that reveals his heart and sets the tone for his leadership. God appears to Solomon and presents him with an extraordinary offer: "Ask what I shall give you" (1 Kings 3:5). Solomon, recognizing the weight of the task before him, does not ask for wealth, power, or long life. Instead, he requests wisdom to govern God's people justly: "Give your servant a discerning heart to govern your people and to distinguish between right and wrong" (1 Kings 3:9).

This pivotal moment is the foundation upon which Solomon's early success is built. His request pleases God, who grants him not only wisdom but also riches, honor, and peace. Solomon's wisdom soon becomes legendary, as seen in his well-known judgment between two women claiming the same child (1 Kings 3:16-28). His ability to discern the truth in that situation reveals a wisdom that transcends mere human intellect—it is divine insight rooted in a heart aligned with God's will.

However, Solomon's story offers us more than an example of successful leadership. It serves as a reminder that wisdom, while a gift from God, must be continually nurtured by obedience and humility. Early in his reign, Solomon demonstrates a deep dependence on God, seeking wisdom not for selfish gain but to serve others. This humility sets him apart, but it also presents a warning: Even the wisest of leaders can fall if they lose sight of God's commandments.

As we reflect on Solomon's request for wisdom, we must ask ourselves: In our own lives, are we seeking wisdom from God, and are we using it to serve His purposes? True wisdom comes from a relationship with God and is always accompanied by a heart that seeks His will above all else. Solomon's early reign illustrates the blessings that flow from such wisdom, but it also foreshadows the danger of allowing success to lead to self-reliance.

The Temple: A New Eden and a Promise of Restoration

One of Solomon's most enduring legacies is the construction of the Temple in Jerusalem. This monumental achievement was more than a political or architectural triumph—it was the fulfillment of a divine promise. God had spoken to David, Solomon's father, and declared that David's son would build a house for His name (2 Samuel 7:12-13). Solomon's Temple became the dwelling place of the Ark of the Covenant, the symbol of God's presence among His people.

But the Temple was more than just a physical structure. In its design, the Temple echoed the imagery of the Garden of Eden, where humanity had once lived in perfect communion with God. The intricate carvings of palm trees, flowers, and cherubim (1 Kings 6:29) served as reminders of that original paradise. The Temple, like Eden, was a place where heaven and earth met, where God's presence dwelled in the midst of His people. It symbolized a new beginning, a restoration of the relationship that had been broken by sin.

The Temple's innermost sanctuary, the Holy of Holies, housed the Ark of the Covenant. It was here, behind a thick veil, that the high priest would enter once a year to make atonement for the sins of the people (Leviticus 16:15-17). The veil represented the separation between God and humanity, a separation that had existed since the fall of Adam and Eve. But even in this separation, the Temple held a promise—a glimpse of the future when God would once again dwell fully with His people, no longer separated by sin.

Solomon's Temple also pointed forward to Jesus Christ, the ultimate fulfillment of God's plan for reconciliation. The sacrificial system practiced in the Temple foreshadowed the perfect sacrifice of Christ, the Lamb of God, who would take away the sins of the world (John 1:29). When Jesus died on the cross, the veil in the Temple was torn from top to bottom (Matthew 27:51), signifying that the barrier between God and humanity had been removed. Through Christ, we have direct access to God's presence, and the need for sacrifices is fulfilled in His once-and-for-all atonement (Hebrews 10:10).

The Temple, then, is not merely an ancient building—it is a symbol of God's desire to restore humanity to Himself. As we reflect on the significance of the Temple, we are reminded that God longs to dwell among His people, and He has made a way for us to be in His presence through the sacrifice of Jesus Christ.

But this reflection also invites us to examine our own lives: Are we cultivating spaces where God's presence can dwell? Just as the Temple was a sacred place where heaven and earth met, our lives are meant to be places where we encounter God daily. How are we creating environments—both physical and spiritual—that invite God's presence into our hearts, homes, and communities?

Prosperity and Peace: Blessings and Temptations

Under Solomon's rule, Israel experienced a period of unparalleled prosperity and peace. Solomon's wisdom attracted traders, dignitaries, and kings from distant lands, bringing wealth and influence to the nation (1 Kings 10:23-25). The Queen of Sheba's visit is a testament to the global reputation Solomon had cultivated: "How happy your people must be! How happy your officials, who continually stand before you and hear your wisdom!" (1 Kings 10:8). The nation thrived, expanding its borders and enjoying security on all sides.

However, with this prosperity came new temptations. The very blessings that God had bestowed upon Solomon became a double-edged sword. The wealth and influence that poured into Israel opened the door to foreign alliances, and with those alliances came foreign gods. The seeds of spiritual compromise were sown in the midst of abundance, and over time, those seeds would take root and bear bitter fruit.

This period of prosperity serves as both a celebration of God's favor and a cautionary tale. Success and abundance can easily lead to spiritual complacency. As Solomon's wealth and power grew, so too did the subtle temptations that would eventually lead him astray. His story reminds us that while prosperity is a blessing from God, it can also become a stumbling block if we lose sight of the One who provides it.

In our own lives, we must ask: Are we allowing the blessings we receive to draw us closer to God, or are they creating distance between us and Him? Prosperity should inspire gratitude and dependence on God, not self-reliance or indulgence. Solomon's reign teaches us that the greatest danger often comes not in times of adversity but in times of abundance.

The Seeds of Idolatry: A Heart Led Astray

Despite the wisdom and blessings Solomon received, his later years were marked by a tragic spiritual decline. Influenced by his many foreign wives, Solomon began to worship foreign gods and allowed idolatry to infiltrate Israel (1 Kings 11:1-8). What began as political alliances grew into spiritual compromises, as Solomon built altars to the gods of his wives and permitted the worship of idols in the land God had set apart for Himself.

Solomon's fall into idolatry reveals a deeper issue—a heart that had gradually drifted from God. The man who had once prayed for wisdom to lead God's people now found himself entangled in the worship of false gods; his heart no longer fully devoted to the Lord. This spiritual drift did not happen overnight; it was the result of small compromises made over time, each one drawing him further away from the God who had granted him such wisdom.

The consequences of Solomon's idolatry were severe. After his death, the kingdom of Israel was divided into two: the northern kingdom of Israel and the southern kingdom of Judah. This division marked the beginning of a long period of turmoil, rebellion, and eventual exile. Solomon's story serves as a powerful reminder that even the wisest among us can be led astray if we are not vigilant in our devotion to God.

Are we guarding our hearts against the subtle temptations that seek to lead us away from God? Solomon's downfall teaches us that the greatest threats to our faith are often not external but internal. It is the slow drift of the heart that leads to spiritual ruin.

Solomon's Legacy: A Pathway to Restoration

Despite Solomon's failures, his legacy remains deeply intertwined with God's plan for restoration. The Temple he built in Jerusalem became a lasting symbol of God's desire to dwell with His people, and it pointed forward to the ultimate restoration that would come through Jesus Christ. Solomon's story, though marked by failure, is also a story of hope. It reminds us that even in our brokenness, God's promises remain steadfast.

The prophets who came after Solomon would call Israel back to covenant faithfulness, but they would also speak of a future King from David's line—one who would reign with righteousness and bring about the full restoration of God's people. This future King is Jesus Christ, the true Son of David, who fulfills the promise of an eternal kingdom (2 Samuel 7:16). Through Him, the division caused by sin is healed, and the way is made for all people to be reconciled to God.

As we reflect on Solomon's legacy, we are reminded that God's redemptive plan is never thwarted by human failure. Even in our worst moments, God is at work, bringing about His purposes for restoration and renewal. Where in your life have you seen failure? Solomon's story invites us to return to God, knowing that He is always ready to restore us when we turn back to Him.

The Role of the Prophets and the Coming King

Although Solomon's reign ended in spiritual decline, it laid the groundwork for the future role of the prophets. As Israel continued to struggle with idolatry and rebellion, the prophets arose to call the people back to their covenant with God. But the prophets did more than call for repentance; they also pointed forward to a coming Messiah, a King from David's line who would reign forever with justice and peace.

This hope finds its fulfillment in Jesus Christ, the ultimate King who restores not only Israel but all of creation. Through His life, death, and resurrection, Jesus tore the veil that separated humanity from God, bringing about the restoration that the Temple had symbolized for generations.

The Road to Restoration

Solomon's reign stands as both a pinnacle of Israel's history and a cautionary tale of spiritual drift. His story illustrates the interplay of divine blessing, human responsibility, and the continual need for reconciliation with God. As we reflect on his legacy, let us carry forward the lessons from his life—seeking wisdom, cultivating sacred spaces, and striving for faithfulness in all we do. The road to restoration is long, but with each step, we draw closer to God's ultimate plan for redemption, which finds its fulfillment in Christ.

As we move beyond Solomon's reign, we enter a time of national division and spiritual decline. Yet, even in the darkest moments, God's promises remained. In the next chapter, we will explore how the prophets played a critical role in calling Israel back to covenant faithfulness and how their messages pointed forward to the coming of the true King—Jesus Christ, who would bring lasting restoration and peace to all creation.

Isaiah 53: 5

But He was pierced for our transgressions; He was crushed for our iniquities; upon Him was the chastisement that brought us peace, and with his wounds we are healed.

Chapter 25 - The Prophets: Hope of a New Covenant

As we move beyond the reign of King Solomon, we enter a period in Israel's history marked by turmoil, spiritual decline, and hope—the era of the prophets. This time was pivotal in God's divine plan, as He raised up prophets to call Israel back to Himself, warning them of the consequences of their rebellion yet always offering the hope of restoration. The prophets were not merely foretellers of events; they were crucial instruments in God's ongoing work of reconciliation and redemption. Their messages carried the weight of divine truth, speaking into the very heart of God's relationship with His people.

The prophets' role was integral to God's overarching plan for humanity. They were tasked with revealing God's character—His justice, mercy, and faithfulness. Their warnings were not simply to punish Israel for sin but to guide them back to the covenant relationship God had established. Through their visions and proclamations, they pointed forward to the ultimate solution for human sin and separation: the coming of the Messiah, who would bring a new covenant, fulfilling God's plan for redemption.

The Heart of the Prophets: Burdened by Their Calling

To understand the role of the prophets, we must first appreciate the weight of their calling. They were not merely messengers but active participants in God's redemptive plan. Chosen by God, these men and women stood in the gap between a holy God and a wayward nation. Their words were often met with hostility, rejection, and personal sacrifice. Yet, their burden was not only to convey warnings but to remind Israel of God's steadfast love and His desire for restoration.

Jeremiah, often called the "weeping prophet," felt the deep sorrow of Israel's brokenness. His grief mirrored God's anguish over His people's sin and rebellion. Jeremiah's tears were not just human emotion; they reflected the heart of God, who longed for His people to return to Him. Similarly, Isaiah's transformative vision of God in the temple (Isaiah 6) underscores the profound experience that empowered the prophets to speak with authority. After being cleansed of his sin, Isaiah willingly responded to God's call: "Here am I. Send me!" (Isaiah 6:8). This encounter demonstrates that the prophets were not merely relaying information; they were part of God's active pursuit of His people.

Each prophet had a personal encounter with God that equipped them for their role in His divine plan. They did not speak on their own authority but were commissioned by God to lead Israel back to Him, to restore what had been broken by sin. Their task was not just to reveal judgment but to offer a pathway to repentance and renewal. Their lives and messages remind us of the seriousness of sin, but also of God's relentless pursuit of His people.

A Call to Repentance: Confronting Injustice and Idolatry

At the core of the prophets' message was a call to repentance. Israel had abandoned their covenant relationship with God, succumbing to idolatry and moral decay. The prophets did not merely condemn these sins—they called for a return to righteousness and justice, two central elements of God's covenant. Through their warnings, the prophets reminded Israel of their unique role as God's chosen people and their responsibility to reflect His character to the nations.

Consider the words of Amos, who boldly confronted the leaders of Israel for their exploitation of the poor and corruption of justice. "Let justice roll down like waters, and righteousness like an ever-flowing stream" (Amos 5:24), he declared, urging the people to understand that true worship could not exist apart from social justice. Amos's call was a reminder that living in covenant with God required both personal holiness and societal righteousness.

The prophets were also relentless in confronting Israel's idolatry. Time and again, the people had turned to foreign gods, breaking their covenant with Yahweh. The prophets likened this idolatry to spiritual adultery—betraying the God who had lovingly redeemed them. Hosea's life itself became a living parable of this truth as God commanded him to marry a prostitute, symbolizing Israel's unfaithfulness. Yet, even in their infidelity, the prophets' message was clear: God was willing to forgive, to heal, and to restore if they would only turn back to Him.

In confronting both injustice and idolatry, the prophets underscored the nature of Israel's sin. Their warnings were not just about breaking commandments; they were about breaking God's heart. They remind us that sin is not merely a violation of law—it is a betrayal of relationship. Yet, in their calls for repentance, we also see the heart of God's divine plan: to bring His people back into right relationship with Him.

Visions of Hope: A New Covenant on the Horizon

Even as the prophets called for repentance, they never left the people without hope. Interwoven with their messages of judgment were promises of restoration—a future where God would renew His covenant with Israel in a transformative way. This new covenant would not be like the old one, written on tablets of stone and dependent on the people's obedience. Instead, it would be written on their hearts, a relationship rooted in grace and empowered by God's Spirit.

Jeremiah spoke powerfully of this new covenant, proclaiming that "I will put my law within them, and I will write it on their hearts. And I will be their God, and they shall be my people" (Jeremiah 31:33). This was a radical shift. No longer would the covenant rely solely on human effort. God Himself would bring about the internal transformation necessary for His people to live in faithfulness. The new covenant would fulfill God's ultimate plan to restore not just Israel but all of humanity.

Ezekiel echoed this hope, envisioning a time when God would give His people new hearts and place His Spirit within them (Ezekiel 36:26-27). This was more than just moral reformation; it was a promise of spiritual renewal. The prophets foretold that God's divine plan for restoration would come to full fruition through the Messiah—through Jesus Christ, who would establish this new covenant by His blood (Luke 22:20).

These promises of hope, spoken centuries before Christ's coming, reveal the consistency of God's plan. Even in the darkest moments of Israel's history, God was preparing the way for a Savior who would bring permanent reconciliation. The prophets saw a future where God's relationship with His people would be restored—not through sacrifices or rituals, but through the work of the coming Messiah.

The Prophets' Role in God's Divine Plan

The prophets were essential players in God's redemptive plan. Through them, God communicated His desire for restoration and His plan to redeem humanity from sin. They were not only spokespeople for God's immediate concerns with Israel's sin and rebellion; they were also heralds of the coming Messiah. Their words pointed forward to Jesus, the fulfillment of the law and the prophets, who would bring about the new covenant and establish God's kingdom on earth.

By calling the people to repentance, the prophets maintained the continuity of God's covenant with Israel, preserving their identity as His chosen people. Through their visions of hope, they provided glimpses of the future restoration that God had planned for all of creation. Their role was pivotal in maintaining the trajectory of God's plan—from creation to the ultimate redemption found in Christ.

Without the prophets, the people of Israel might have been entirely lost in their sin and rebellion. But through the prophets, God kept His promise to remain faithful, always holding out the offer of restoration. The prophets were the bridge between the old covenant and the new, between the brokenness of humanity and the wholeness that would come through Christ.

The New Covenant: Fulfillment in Christ

The promises of the prophets ultimately find their fulfillment in the coming of Jesus Christ. Through Him, the new covenant was established—a covenant not based on human effort but on God's grace. In Christ, the law was no longer external, written on stone tablets, but internal, written on the hearts of His people. His life, death, and resurrection provided the way for the reconciliation that the prophets had long foretold.

Jesus fulfilled the prophets' visions of justice, mercy, and restoration. He embodied the righteousness they called for, and His sacrifice on the cross made possible the full realization of the new covenant. In Him, the prophetic promises of a restored relationship between God and His people came to pass.

The Longing for the Messiah: Fulfilled in Jesus

For centuries, the people of Israel waited for the fulfillment of the prophets' words. Even during the four hundred years of silence between the last of the Old Testament prophets and the birth of Christ, the hope of a coming Messiah remained alive. When Jesus was born in Bethlehem, the silence was broken, and the long-awaited promise was fulfilled. The prophets had longed for this day—the day when God's ultimate plan for reconciliation would come to fruition.

In Christ, the long-awaited new covenant was established. Through His life, He perfectly fulfilled the law and the prophets. Through His death, He offered Himself as the ultimate sacrifice, fulfilling the promises of the prophets and making a way for humanity to be reconciled to God. In His resurrection, He secured the hope of eternal life for all who believe.

Final Reflections: The Prophets and God's Divine Plan

The prophets were not just figures of the past. They were pivotal instruments in God's unfolding plan of redemption. Through their words, their warnings, and their visions, they prepared the way for the coming of the Messiah and the establishment of the new covenant. Their role was to call Israel back to faithfulness, but also to reveal God's unchanging desire to restore all of humanity to Himself.

As we reflect on their messages, let us be reminded that the hope they proclaimed is now our reality in Christ. We are the recipients of the new covenant—the fulfillment of God's redemptive plan. Let their words inspire us to live as people of this covenant, continually seeking to reflect God's love, justice, and mercy in the world.

As we leave the era of the prophets, we now turn to the one who fulfilled their words—Jesus Christ. In the next chapter, we will explore how Christ's life and ministry brought about the fulfillment of the new covenant, offering redemption and restoration to all of creation.

Chapter 26 - The Coming of the Messiah: Jesus and the Fulfillment of Promise

As we journeyed through the Old Testament, from the covenant with Abraham to the prophetic words that sustained Israel's hope, we witnessed the unfolding of God's divine plan for restoration. Each covenant, every moment of deliverance, and each prophetic message revealed more of God's redemptive purpose. The promises made to Abraham, the Law given through Moses, and the hope declared by the prophets all pointed to one central figure: the Messiah, who would reconcile humanity to God.

Now, in the person of Jesus Christ, the Messiah, we arrive at the culmination of this divine plan. His coming fulfills centuries of longing and expectation. From the moment God promised a Savior in the Garden of Eden to the covenant with Abraham that his descendants would bless the nations, to the prophetic cries for a Redeemer—each step has been leading to this one pivotal event: the arrival of Jesus, who would restore humanity's broken relationship with God.

Jesus' birth, life, death, and resurrection stand at the center of God's redemptive story. He is the one through whom all the promises of Scripture find their fulfillment. In Jesus, God's plan for restoration is fully revealed, offering hope not only to Israel but to the entire world. As we reflect on His life and ministry, we witness the fullness of God's faithfulness and His profound love for creation.

The Birth of the Messiah: A New Beginning

Imagine the scene: a star-lit night, the quiet countryside, and a baby wrapped in swaddling clothes lying in a manger. The angel's words still echo: "For unto you is born this day in the city of David a Savior, who is Christ the Lord" (Luke 2:11). This moment was not just the birth of a child; it marked the beginning of the long-awaited restoration, the fulfillment of God's promises.

Jesus' birth was prophesied centuries before by the prophets. Micah foretold that the Messiah would be born in Bethlehem (Micah 5:2), and Isaiah spoke of a virgin bearing a son who would be called Emmanuel— "God with us" (Isaiah 7:14). In this humble moment, God entered His creation, becoming flesh to dwell among humanity (John 1:14). His arrival was a vivid reminder that God had not abandoned His people but was actively working to restore the broken relationship between humanity and Himself.

This was not merely the birth of a historical figure. Jesus' birth signified the fulfillment of God's covenant with Israel and the beginning of a new covenant that would extend to all people. The hope of restoration, once whispered by the prophets, was now being fulfilled in the cries of a newborn King.

The Life and Ministry of Jesus: God's Presence Among Us

Jesus' ministry was the embodiment of God's love and grace in action. He preached about the Kingdom of God, calling all people to repentance while exemplifying what it means to live in alignment with God's design. Through His miracles and acts of compassion, Jesus revealed God's heart for the marginalized and oppressed, showing that the Kingdom was inclusive—not just for Israel but for all who would believe.

The miracles He performed fulfilled the prophecies of Isaiah, who proclaimed that the Messiah would heal the sick and bring sight to the blind (Isaiah 61:1; 42:7). But these acts of healing were more than demonstrations of power; they were signs of God's Kingdom breaking into the world, a tangible expression of the restoration Jesus had come to bring. Each miracle pointed to the ultimate restoration of creation, where sin, death, and suffering would be no more.

His teachings, often conveyed through parables, explained the nature of this Kingdom. Jesus invited people into a transformative relationship with God, urging them to live out the values of the Kingdom—love, forgiveness, and humility. Consider His interaction with the Samaritan woman at the well or Zacchaeus the tax collector—each encounter demonstrated God's relentless pursuit of humanity, showing that no one is beyond the reach of His grace.

Jesus didn't just preach about restoration; He lived it. Every act of mercy, every word of forgiveness, and every healing was a foretaste of the greater restoration to come. Through His life, Jesus embodied the hope that God's promises were coming to fruition.

The Death of the Messiah: The Ultimate Sacrifice

As Jesus' mission unfolded, it became clear that His purpose would culminate at the cross. His death was not a tragic accident; it was the fulfillment of God's plan for atonement and reconciliation. At the Last Supper, Jesus established a new covenant with His disciples, declaring, "This cup that is poured out for you is the new covenant in my blood" (Luke 22:20). This covenant was a promise that His death would be the means by which humanity's broken relationship with God could be restored.

On the cross, Jesus bore the sins of the world, fulfilling the role of the Passover Lamb (John 1:29). His sacrificial death accomplished what the sacrifices of the Old Covenant could not: the full and final atonement for sin. His words, "It is finished" (John 19:30), marked the completion of His mission. The temple veil was torn in two (Matthew 27:51), symbolizing the removal of the barrier that had long separated humanity from God. Through His death, Jesus opened the way for all people to have access to God.

The cross is the ultimate expression of God's love and commitment to restoring His creation. Jesus' death was the turning point in human history, where the power of sin and death was broken and the door to reconciliation was opened.

The Resurrection: Victory Over Sin and Death

Three days after His death, Jesus rose from the grave, marking the ultimate victory over sin and death. His resurrection was not just a sign of His power; it was the confirmation that God's plan for restoration was being fulfilled. When the angel declared, "He is not here, but has risen" (Luke 24:6), it was the proclamation of new life and hope.

Through His resurrection, Jesus not only conquered death but also inaugurated the new creation. Paul calls Jesus the "firstfruits" of those who have died, meaning His resurrection is the guarantee of our future resurrection (1 Corinthians 15:20). In rising from the dead, Jesus brought the promise of eternal life and confirmed that God's restoration plan was not just a spiritual reality but also a physical one.

The resurrection ensures that the power of sin is broken and that all who believe in Christ will experience eternal life. Through His victory, the hope of restoration is no longer a distant promise but a present reality for all who place their faith in Him.

The Ongoing Promise of Restoration

Through Jesus, God's promise of restoration extends to all creation. His life, death, and resurrection opened the door for reconciliation, not only for individuals but for the renewal of the entire world. The same God who promised to restore Israel now invites people from every nation to experience a restored relationship with Him. This echoes the covenantal promises made to Abraham, reminding us that God's desire has always been to create a people for Himself from all nations.

As we reflect on the significance of Jesus' work, we see that restoration is not just a personal experience but a cosmic one. God's plan is to redeem all things, to renew all creation, and to bring everything under the Lordship of Christ (Colossians 1:20). The hope of restoration is not only for the individual soul but for the entire world—a world that will one day be made new.

Looking Ahead: The Birth of the Church

As we move into the next chapter, we will witness how the resurrection of Jesus and the coming of the Holy Spirit laid the foundation for the Church. The early believers, empowered by the Spirit, carried forward the mission of Christ—spreading the message of reconciliation and hope to the world. The Church, as the body of Christ on earth, continues the work of restoration, proclaiming the good news of the Kingdom to all nations.

The story of God's restoration didn't end with Jesus' ascension; it continues through His people. The Church is called to embody the message of reconciliation, to be the hands and feet of Christ in a world still longing for healing and restoration.

As we prepare to explore the birth of the Church, let us remember that the themes of love, grace, and reconciliation are not just historical truths but living realities. Through Jesus, the Messiah, the hope of restoration has been fulfilled, and we are invited to be active participants in the ongoing story of redemption.

Acts 1:9

And when he had said these things, as they were looking on, he was lifted up, and a cloud took him out of their sight.

Chapter 27 - The Great Commission: Gods Plan to Restore the Nations

As we continue from the powerful events surrounding Jesus' resurrection, we arrive at a pivotal juncture in God's grand narrative of restoration—a moment that resonates with hope and promise for all humanity. This chapter marks the coming of the Holy Spirit at Pentecost, the birth of the Church, and the unfolding mystery of the inclusion of the Gentiles in God's redemptive plan. These elements not only transformed the early disciples but also laid the groundwork for a global movement dedicated to bringing restoration to the nations.

The Coming of the Holy Spirit: Empowerment for a New Mission

Following His resurrection, Jesus offered His disciples not just reassurance but a profound sense of purpose. Imagine their hearts, still trembling from fear and confusion, as He spoke words of promise: "You will receive power when the Holy Spirit has come upon you, and you will be my witnesses in Jerusalem and in all Judea and Samaria, and to the end of the earth" (Acts 1:8). This moment represented a seismic shift in their mission, echoing throughout the early Church's history and resonating into our lives today.

The Promise of the Holy Spirit: A New Era

The promise of the Holy Spirit was more than just an assurance of divine companionship—it signified a radical transformation in the relationship between God and humanity. Prior to this moment, the Holy Spirit's presence was often fleeting, descending upon individuals chosen for specific tasks. However, through Jesus' resurrection and ascension, a new era dawned where the Holy Spirit would indwell all believers permanently, empowering them to carry out God's mission of restoration.

This shift was essential for several reasons:

Enabling Witnesses: Picture the disciples, once marked by fear and uncertainty, transformed into bold witnesses of Christ's resurrection. Their newfound courage did not come from themselves but from the supernatural empowerment of the Holy Spirit. With this power, they spoke boldly, performed miracles, and endured persecution with grace—all central aspects of their mission and a testament to the Spirit's work within them.

Spiritual Gifts and Unity: Along with the Holy Spirit came a diversity of spiritual gifts, which unified the believers into a cohesive community with a shared mission. In 1 Corinthians 12:4-11, Paul emphasizes how these varied gifts, given by the same Spirit, work together for the common good. This unity in diversity wasn't just an organizational structure—it was vital to the Church's mission, allowing every member to contribute their unique talents to spread the Gospel.

Empowerment for a Global Mission: Jesus' directive to be witnesses "to the end of the earth" underscored the expansive nature of their mission. At Pentecost, the miraculous ability to speak in new languages symbolized God's intention to break down geographical, cultural, and linguistic barriers. This foreshadowed the inclusive nature of His redemptive plan, established long ago with His promises to Abraham and fulfilled in Christ.

The Birth of the Church at Pentecost

The promise Jesus made to His disciples culminated at Pentecost, a significant Jewish festival celebrated fifty days after Passover. The timing was divinely orchestrated, gathering people from various nations in Jerusalem and creating a unique opportunity for the Gospel to be proclaimed to a diverse audience.

In Acts 2, we witness the Holy Spirit descending like a mighty wind, filling the disciples with power to speak in different languages. What an awe-inspiring moment! People from distant lands heard the message of Christ in their own tongues, illustrating God's intentional plan to restore and reconcile all nations through the Gospel.

This moment was not just about the miraculous phenomena—it was a strategic element in God's divine plan. Centuries earlier, the prophet Joel had spoken of a day when God would pour out His Spirit on all flesh (Joel 2:28-29). At Pentecost, this prophecy was fulfilled. The arrival of the Holy Spirit signaled the dawn of a new era where the barriers between nations, cultures, and languages were being broken down, paving the way for God's message of restoration to reach the ends of the earth.

Public Proclamation: The Gospel in Every Tongue

This miraculous event set the stage for Peter's powerful sermon. Filled with the Holy Spirit, Peter boldly proclaimed the death and resurrection of Jesus, linking these events to the fulfillment of Old Testament prophecies. His words pierced the hearts of those who listened, resulting in approximately three thousand conversions in a single day (Acts 2:41). This was the birth of the Church—a global community of believers charged with carrying forth God's mission of reconciliation to the world.

Establishing Community: A New Kind of Family

The events of Pentecost did more than birth the Church; they created a new type of community, bound by faith in Christ and the empowerment of the Holy Spirit. The early Church devoted themselves to the apostles' teachings, fellowship, breaking of bread, and prayer (Acts 2:42). This communal life emphasized shared faith and mutual support, essential as they embarked on their mission to reach all nations.

God's orchestration of Pentecost revealed His deep desire to restore humanity and draw all peoples into His covenant family. By empowering the disciples to communicate in the languages of those present, He broke down cultural and linguistic barriers, setting the stage for a global movement that would extend His message of love, grace, and reconciliation across the earth.

A Crucial Step in God's Redemptive Plan

The arrival of the Holy Spirit at Pentecost was a pivotal step in God's overarching plan to restore and reconcile humanity. It fulfilled the prophecies of a new covenant, a theme woven throughout Scripture, from God's promises to Abraham to the culmination found in the life, death, and resurrection of Christ.

A New Covenant: In Jeremiah 31:31-34, God promised a new covenant, writing His law on the hearts of His people. The arrival of the Holy Spirit signified the initiation of this covenant, enabling believers to live in relationship with God—not out of obligation, but from transformed hearts filled with love.

The Restoration of Creation: Throughout Scripture, God's longing to restore all creation is clear. The coming of the Holy Spirit marks the beginning of this restoration process, equipping believers to bring hope, healing, and the transformative message of the Gospel to all people.

The Holy Spirit's arrival at Pentecost empowered a diverse and united body of believers to carry the message of Christ to the ends of the earth, fulfilling God's promise and initiating the restoration of all creation. This moment serves as a powerful reminder that, through divine empowerment, fear can be transformed into boldness, isolation into community, and limitation into limitless mission.

Fulfilling the Great Commission: The Call to Action

The Great Commission, recorded in Matthew 28:19-20, compels believers to "Go therefore and make disciples of all nations, baptizing them in the name of the Father and of the Son and of the Holy Spirit." This charge reflects the global scope of God's plan and the Church's responsibility to carry the Gospel to every corner of the earth.

From the covenant with Abraham to the commissioning of the apostles, God's plan has always been to bring restoration to the nations. The Great Commission is not just a task but the culmination of a divine promise to reach the entire world, breaking down barriers of ethnicity, nationality, and culture to create one global family united in Christ.

The Mystery of Inclusion: Gentiles and the Gospel

The inclusion of the Gentiles was a revolutionary concept for the early Church. The account of Peter and Cornelius in Acts 10 illustrates this radical shift in understanding. God revealed to Peter that "what God has made clean, do not call common" (Acts 10:15), leading to the baptism of the first Gentile believer. This marked a significant moment in grasping God's redemptive plan: salvation through Christ was not limited to the Jewish people but extended to all who believe.

The Apostle Paul further articulated this mystery in his letters, emphasizing that through Christ, both Jews and Gentiles are united as one body, reconciled to God and to each other (Ephesians 2:14-16). The Church's mission transformed into one of proclamation and action, demonstrating that God's love and grace are accessible to all—a continuation of the hope expressed throughout the preceding chapters.

The Gospel's Power: Transforming Lives and Communities

As the early Church spread the Gospel, countless lives were transformed, and entire communities changed. Acts 2:47 states, "And the Lord added to their number day by day those who were being saved." This growth signifies that the Gospel carries the power to heal and restore—a reality that continues to this day.

In a world burdened by sin, division, and despair, the Church remains a vessel of hope, embodying the heart of God's restoration plan. The mission entrusted to believers is not just a task; it is a call to partner with God in the work of healing the brokenness that permeates our world.

The Continuing Journey of Restoration

As we reflect on this chapter, the depth of God's plan for restoration comes into clearer focus. It's not just an ancient story to admire—it's a living narrative that continues, and we are all part of it. The coming of the Holy Spirit at Pentecost and the birth of the Church are landmarks in God's unwavering commitment to restore His creation. Generation after generation, God invites us to take our place in this redemptive work.

At Pentecost, heaven touched earth in a way that forever changed human history. Those early believers, still grappling with confusion and grief, stood on the brink of something beyond their understanding. Jesus had promised them power, but could they have imagined what that truly meant? When the Holy Spirit descended, their lives were transformed. Fear and doubt gave way to boldness and purpose as they became the Church—the body of Christ, called to continue His work on earth.

An Invitation to Join the Story

The same Spirit that empowered the early disciples is the Spirit that lives in us today. Just like those first disciples, you are empowered. The same Holy Spirit that filled them with boldness and transformed their lives is at work in you.

As we continue this journey of faith, the Great Commission is not just a story from history—it's an ongoing invitation to us today. We are called to step into our communities and beyond, empowered by the Holy Spirit, to share the hope of restoration that we have found in Christ.

Hebrews 10:25

Not neglecting to meet together, as is the habit of some, but encouraging one another, and all the more as you see the Day drawing near..

Matthew 24: 6-8

You will hear of wars and rumors of wars, but see to it that you are not alarmed. Such things must happen, but the end is still to come. Nation will rise against nation, and kingdom against kingdom. There will be famines and earthquakes in various places. All these are the beginning of birth pains.

Chapter 28 – From Judgement to Glory: The Tribulation and Christ's Return

As we transition from the Great Commission and the establishment of the early Church, we arrive at a pivotal and climactic moment in God's divine plan: the Tribulation. For centuries, this period has been anticipated, filled with both dread and hope. The Tribulation marks not only the judgment of the earth but also an extraordinary opportunity for redemption. It is the moment when God's promises of restoration, made to Israel and the nations, begin to reach their fulfillment.

In this chapter, we will explore the Tribulation, the rapture of the Church, and how these events weave into God's ultimate plan. This is more than just a theological framework—it is deeply personal and essential to our understanding of God's redemptive timeline.

The Rapture of the Church: A Divine Gathering

Before the Tribulation unfolds, Scripture speaks of a remarkable event for believers—the Rapture. This is not merely an item on a prophetic calendar but a profound promise of hope. The Apostle Paul, in his letter to the Thessalonians, offers a vivid and comforting vision: "For the Lord Himself will descend from heaven with a cry of command, with the voice of an archangel, and with the sound of the trumpet of God. And the dead in Christ will rise first" (1 Thessalonians 4:16). Imagine that moment—the trumpet sounding, the skies parting, and the Lord descending, not in judgment but to gather His Church.

This moment marks the close of the Church Age and the beginning of a new chapter in God's plan. Believers are caught up to be with Christ, while the focus shifts back to Israel, fulfilling God's promises to the nation. Even as God's wrath is about to be poured out on the world,

His mercy shines through. This promise of the Rapture is a reminder of God's faithfulness, not just to the Church but to all who will trust in His name.

The Timing of the Rapture: Different Perspectives

The timing of the Rapture in relation to the Tribulation has been debated for centuries. While there are differing views, all agree on one central truth: Christ will come for His Church. Let's briefly look at the three main perspectives:

Pre-Tribulation View: This view holds that the Rapture occurs before the seven-year Tribulation begins. Believers are taken up to heaven, spared from the coming judgment. This is supported by passages such as 1 Thessalonians 5:9, which says, "For God has not destined us for wrath but to obtain salvation through our Lord Jesus Christ."

Mid-Tribulation View: This perspective suggests that the Rapture happens midway through the Tribulation, just before the "Great Tribulation," the final and most intense period of judgment. Proponents often point to Revelation 11, where the seventh trumpet is sounded, signaling the completion of certain judgments and the gathering of God's people.

Post-Tribulation View: This view teaches that the Rapture occurs at the end of the Tribulation, just before Christ's second coming. Believers go through the Tribulation but are spiritually protected. As Christ returns, the Church is caught up to meet Him in the air, joining Him as He establishes His Kingdom.

Regardless of when the Rapture occurs, the core truth remains: Jesus will return for His Church, and we will be with Him forever. His promise is sure, and His faithfulness to us will endure, whether we are spared from the Tribulation or go through parts of it.

The Seven Years of Tribulation: Wrath and Redemption

The Tribulation is a time like no other in history—a period marked by intense judgment but also extraordinary mercy. It's a time of reckoning for a world that has rejected God, but also a time when His grace will still be extended to those who turn to Him. Jesus described the Tribulation as a period of unprecedented suffering: "For then there will be great tribulation, such as has not been from the beginning of the world until now" (Matthew 24:21).

The seven years of Tribulation are divided into two parts. The first half sees the rise of the Antichrist, deception, and mounting chaos. The second half, known as the "Great Tribulation," is when God's judgments intensify, and the Antichrist demands to be worshiped as God. Yet, even amid the devastation, God's mercy is evident. He will give the world one final chance to turn to Him.

This period also holds special significance for Israel. During the Tribulation, God will bring Israel to the forefront of His plan, awakening many to the truth of Jesus as their Messiah. The Tribulation, while a time of judgment, is also a time of divine mercy, offering a last call for repentance and restoration.

Daniel's Seventy Weeks: Understanding the Prophetic Timeline

To understand the Tribulation more fully, we must look back at the prophecy of Daniel's seventy weeks (Daniel 9:24-27). This prophecy lays out God's timeline for Israel and the world, with seventy "weeks" (or sets of seven years) that guide the unfolding of His plan. The first sixty-nine weeks were completed with the coming of Jesus, who was "cut off" at His crucifixion.

But one week remains—the final seven years, which correspond to the Tribulation. This is the period during which God's focus will return to Israel, completing His promises to them. The Tribulation is the final act in a long, redemptive drama, where Israel's story is fully restored.

Israel's Restoration: Fulfillment of God's Promises

While the Tribulation is a time of global judgment, it is also a time of incredible restoration for Israel. Scripture speaks of 144,000 being sealed from the tribes of Israel—a remnant chosen to proclaim the truth of Christ during this time (Revelation 7:4). Through their witness, many in Israel will come to faith in Jesus as their Messiah.

Zechariah prophesied about this day: "They will call upon my name, and I will answer them. I will say, 'They are my people'; and they will say, 'The Lord is my God'" (Zechariah 13:9). The nation of Israel, after centuries of spiritual estrangement, will be restored to their rightful place in God's plan. This restoration is a powerful testament to God's unrelenting love and faithfulness to His covenant people.

The Divine Purpose: Judgment and Mercy in Tandem

Throughout the Tribulation, God's judgment and mercy work in tandem. His judgments are severe, but His hand remains extended to those who will turn to Him. Even in the darkest moments of human history, God's grace shines through. Paul reminds us that "God has not rejected His people" (Romans 11:2), and this truth reverberates throughout the Tribulation as God seeks to redeem both Israel and the nations.

God's ultimate purpose in the Tribulation is to prepare the world for Christ's return. This period cleanses the earth of evil and sets the stage for the final act of redemption—when Christ will come again, not as the suffering servant, but as the victorious King.

Looking Forward: The King's Return

As we look ahead, the Tribulation is not the end of the story. It is a necessary chapter that leads to the return of Jesus Christ in glory. When He returns, He will establish His Kingdom on earth, fulfilling every

Creation, Rebellion and God's Plan for Restoration

promise He has made. This moment will mark the restoration of not only Israel but all of creation.

The next chapter will explore this glorious return of Christ, the establishment of His Kingdom, and the fulfillment of God's ultimate plan. The Tribulation is a time of judgment, but it is also a time of hope—hope that the return of the King is drawing near, and with it, the renewal of all things.

Revelation 11:15

Then the seventh angel blew his trumpet, and there were loud voices in heaven, saying, "The kingdom of the world has become the kingdom of our Lord and of his Christ, and he shall reign forever and ever."

Chapter 29 - Restoration Complete: The Kingdom and the Renewal of Creation

As we come to the culmination of our journey, we stand at the threshold of the most profound and awe-inspiring event in the history of creation: the return of Jesus Christ and the restoration of all things. This is not just the end of a long and complex story—it is the glorious beginning of eternity. We have walked through the pages of Scripture together, tracing God's plan for humanity from the moment of creation through the fall, the covenants, the coming of Christ, and the establishment of the Church. Now, at last, we arrive at the ultimate fulfillment of God's redemptive work: the renewal of all creation under Christ's eternal reign.

Christ's Return in Glory: The King Comes Back

The Second Coming of Christ is the climactic event of God's divine plan—a moment that will shake the foundations of heaven and earth. Jesus, who first came in humility as a servant and Savior, will return as a triumphant King, clothed in power and majesty. In Matthew 24:30, we are told, "Then will appear in heaven the sign of the Son of Man, and then all the tribes of the earth will mourn, and they will see the Son of Man coming on the clouds of heaven with power and great glory."

Can you envision it? The skies splitting open, the heavens resounding with the trumpet call, and Christ descending in radiant glory. It will be a moment unlike any other in history—visible to all, unmistakable in its significance. This is the fulfillment of every prophecy, the answer to every prayer, and the realization of every hope. For believers, this is the moment we have longed for, the culmination of our faith, when every tear is wiped away, every pain healed, and every wrong made right. Christ's return is not merely an event to be observed; it is a cosmic turning point where justice, righteousness, and love will reign supreme.

But Christ's return is not only about triumph; it is also about transformation. The world as we know it—broken, fallen, and scarred by sin—will be restored to its original purpose. The curse that began in the Garden of Eden will be undone, and a new creation will emerge, radiant with the glory of God. In this renewed world, Christ will reign as King, and His people will dwell with Him forever.

The Judgment: A Moment of Reckoning

Following Christ's return, we face the sobering reality of the final judgment—a moment when every person and every nation will stand before the throne of God. This is a time of accountability, where the choices we have made and the lives we have lived will be brought into the light of His justice. Yet, it is also a moment filled with mercy, as Christ's perfect righteousness covers those who have trusted in Him.

In Matthew 25:31-32, Jesus describes this scene: "When the Son of Man comes in His glory, and all the angels with Him, then He will sit on His glorious throne. Before Him will be gathered all the nations, and He will separate people one from another as a shepherd separates the sheep from the goats." The judgment is not just about condemnation—it is about God's ultimate justice. For those who have embraced His grace, it is the entrance into eternal life and the joy of His presence. For others, it is the final reckoning, a confrontation with the consequences of rejecting God's offer of salvation.

This moment of judgment also marks the restoration of the nations. God's plan has always been global in scope. The nations scattered at Babel will be brought together in Christ. Every tribe, tongue, and people will be represented, and God will establish His Kingdom as the true and final ruler of all. For Israel, this judgment also marks a profound moment of restoration, as God fulfills His ancient promises to the nation and restores them to a place of honor in His Kingdom.

The Restoration of Israel

Throughout Scripture, Israel has held a unique place in God's redemptive plan. From the covenant with Abraham to the establishment of David's throne, God's promises to Israel are an integral part of His divine story. In the wake of Christ's return, we will witness the fulfillment of these promises. Romans 11:26 declares, "And in this way all Israel will be saved, as it is written, 'The Deliverer will come from Zion, He will banish ungodliness from Jacob.'"

Imagine the moment when Israel, long estranged and scattered, will be restored. This is the fulfillment of God's covenantal promises—the moment when the people of Israel, the chosen nation, will embrace their Messiah, recognizing Him as the Savior they had once rejected. It is a powerful testimony of God's faithfulness, that even through millennia of rebellion and suffering, His promises to Israel remain unbroken.

But this restoration is not only for Israel—it is a reflection of the wider restoration God has planned for all of humanity. Just as God's covenant with Israel stands as a sign of His commitment to His people, so too does His covenant with the Church, made through the blood of Christ, extend to all who believe. The restoration of Israel is a foretaste of the full renewal of all creation.

The Millennial Kingdom: A Reign of Peace

With Christ's return, the Millennial Kingdom begins—a thousand-year reign of peace and righteousness. This is the moment when the prayers of the faithful are answered, and the world is finally as it was meant to be. Isaiah 11:6 paints a beautiful picture of this time: "The wolf shall dwell with the lamb, and the leopard shall lie down with the young goat... for the earth shall be full of the knowledge of the Lord as the waters cover the sea."

In this Kingdom, the effects of sin are undone. The natural world, which has groaned under the weight of the fall, will be restored. Creation itself will be set free from its bondage to decay and share in the glorious freedom of the children of God (Romans 8:21). Human relationships, too, will be healed. There will be no more war, no more suffering, no more death. Christ will reign in perfect justice and love, and His people will live in His presence, finally experiencing the fullness of life that God always intended.

This is not just a distant hope—it is the destiny for which we are being prepared. Even now, we are called to live as citizens of this coming Kingdom, embodying its values of peace, justice, and mercy in our lives today. As we do so, we become witnesses to the world of the restoration that is yet to come.

The Renewal of Creation

Finally, we arrive at the ultimate promise—the renewal of all creation. In Revelation 21:1, John describes his vision: "Then I saw a new heaven and a new earth, for the first heaven and the first earth had passed away, and the sea was no more." This is the climax of God's plan, the moment when the entire cosmos is remade, free from the corruption and decay that have plagued it since the fall.

Can you picture it? A world without pain, without fear, without death. A world where the beauty of creation reflects the glory of God in ways we can scarcely imagine. Mountains, rivers, forests—all of it renewed, vibrant, and alive with the presence of God. This is the future we are promised—a future where everything that was lost in Eden is restored, where humanity once again walks with God in perfect harmony.

This promise of renewal is not just for the earth—it is for each of us as well. Our bodies, broken by sin and frailty, will be transformed. Our relationships, scarred by division and hurt, will be healed. Our hearts, weighed down by sorrow and fear, will be lifted into the fullness of joy and peace in God's presence. This is the ultimate hope of the Gospel—that through Christ, all things will be made new.

Conclusion: A Lasting Hope for Eternity

As we stand on the brink of eternity, contemplating the promise of Christ's return and the renewal of all creation, let this vision sink deeply into your heart. The fullness of God's love—so vast, so infinite—will one day envelop all creation, healing every broken soul, every scarred place in the world, and making all things new. This is not just the conclusion of a story—it is the eternal beginning of what we were always meant for: perfect communion with God, dwelling in the fullness of His presence forever.

You are not a passive observer in this divine narrative; you are a vital part of God's grand plan. Your life, your choices, and your faithfulness are woven into the fabric of eternity. Every act of love, every moment of faith, every step of obedience is part of God's redemptive story. You are called to be a witness to the hope that is coming, to live as a reflection of Christ's love and grace in a world that desperately needs the light of His Kingdom.

As you move forward from here, carry this hope with you. Let it shape your decisions, your relationships, and your faith. Let it inspire you to be a beacon of light in a world still longing for redemption. And as you wait for that glorious day when Christ returns and all things are made new, live with the knowledge that you are a beloved part of God's eternal plan, and that your story is intricately and beautifully woven into His.

We are not just awaiting an ending—we are living in anticipation of a beginning, an eternity filled with joy, peace, and the presence of God. Together, we look forward to that day when every tear will be wiped away, every sorrow turned to joy, and every part of creation sings in harmony with its Creator.

And so, dear friend, let us journey on with hope and joy in our hearts, actively seeking to reflect Christ's love in our lives. May we remind one another of the beautiful future that awaits us, living in anticipation of the day when God's restoration will be complete, and we will dwell with Him forever, rejoicing in the fullness of His love.

In Christ,

Michael McCullough

References:

Biblical Reference

Bible: English Standard Version (ESV)

Theological Works

A.W. Tozer: The Knowledge of the Holy – Explores God's eternal nature: "God dwells in eternity, but time dwells in God."

Stephen Charnock: The Existence and Attributes of God – Discusses God's infinitude: "If eternity were anything distinct from God... there would be something which was not God, necessary to perfect God."

Michael S. Heiser: The Unseen Realm: Recovering the Supernatural Worldview of the Bible – Insights into the divine council and spiritual realm.

G.K. Beale: The Temple and the Church's Mission – Significance of the heavens as God's dwelling and the role of divine beings.

John H. Walton: The Lost World of Genesis One – Understanding "heavens" in ancient cosmology.

N.T. Wright: Paul and the Faithfulness of God – Theological framework for discussing spiritual authorities.

Gregory A. Boyd: God at War: The Bible & Spiritual Conflict – Examination of spiritual warfare and cosmic authorities.

Wayne Grudem: Systematic Theology – Discusses God's nature and divine love.

John MacArthur: The Love of God – Explores God's love in creation.

J.I. Packer: Knowing God – Insight into God's attributes, including love and purpose.

Creation and Redemption Literature

Colin E. Gunton: The Doctrine of Creation – Relationship between God's creative act and redemption.

Albert M. Wolters: Creation Regained – Purpose of creation in God's redemptive plan.

Commentaries

G.J. Wenham et al.: The New Bible Commentary – Exegesis on creation narratives.

Bruce K. Waltke: Genesis: A Commentary – Insights into the creation narrative and the image of God.

Victor P. Hamilton: The Book of Genesis: Chapters 1-17 – Analysis of Genesis creation accounts.

Henri Blocher: In the Beginning: The Opening Chapters of Genesis – Reflections on the goodness of creation.

James Montgomery Boice: Genesis: An Expositional Commentary – Theological insights on creation.

Richard J. Clifford: Creation Accounts in the Ancient Near East and in the Bible – Comparative studies of creation accounts.

Walter Brueggemann: Genesis: A Theological Commentary – Theological reflections on Genesis.

Nahum M. Sarna: Genesis: The Traditional Hebrew Text – Commentary on narrative structure and themes.

Claus Westermann: Genesis 1-11: A Commentary – Focus on literary and theological interpretations.

Biblical Theology

N.T. Wright: The Day the Revolution Began – Themes of covenant and humanity's role in God's plan.

Scholarly Works

John Barton: The Hebrew Bible: A Critical Companion – Insights into Hebrew language in biblical texts.

David L. Baker: The Serpent: A New Investigation of the Biblical Tradition – Theological significance of the serpent in Genesis.

David E. S. Stein: Satan and the Problem of Evil – Discusses the nature of evil and the role of Satan.

Thomas A. G. Reiner: Eden, the Temple, and the Mountain – Symbolism of Eden and cosmic themes.

Ancient Near Eastern Texts

James B. Pritchard (ed.): Ancient Near Eastern Texts Relating to the Old Testament – Context for creation narratives.

Leonard Woolley: The Ziggurat of Ur – Historical reference for ancient cities and religious practices.

The Epic of Gilgamesh – Insights into ancient Near Eastern cosmology.

Enuma Elish – Context on creation narratives in the ancient Near East.

Historical and Cultural Context

Christopher Rowland: The Open Heaven – Examines Jewish and Christian apocalyptic literature.

Michael A. Lyons: An Introduction to Ezekiel – Contextualizes pride in Ezekiel 28.

Victor H. Matthews: The Cultural World of the Bible – Descriptions of ancient geography and human-divine interaction.

Jodi Magness: The Archaeology of the Holy Land – Insights into ancient sacred landscapes.

Reflection and Application

Henri J. M. Nouwen: The Return of the Prodigal Son – Themes of sin and redemption.

Jürgen Moltmann: The Coming of God: Christian Eschatology – Explores hope of redemption amid moral decay.

Apocryphal and Pseudepigraphal Texts

The Book of Enoch – Elaborates on the rebellion of the "Sons of God."

The Book of Giants – Provides context about the Nephilim.

Articles and Papers

Jonathan L. Wright: "Lucifer, the Serpent, and the Fall: A Study of Biblical Imagery."

Richard J. Bauckham: "Cosmic Warfare in the Old Testament."

Scott Hahn: "The Garden of Eden: A Study in the Theology of the Old Testament."

Richard B. Hays: "The Old Testament in the New: An Exegetical Study."

Linguistic Studies

Francis Brown, Samuel Rolles Driver, and Charles A. Briggs: A Dictionary of Biblical Hebrew and Aramaic – Definitions of Hebrew terms, including "nachash."

Historical and Archaeological References

Etemenanki – Research articles on the ziggurat.

Modern Commentaries

Derek Kidner: Genesis: An Introduction and Commentary – Insights on Genesis 1-11 and God's judgment.

Literary and Cultural Analysis

Frank M. Cross: Canaanite Myth and Hebrew Epic – Explores interactions of Hebrew narratives with surrounding mythologies.

Additional Biblical References

Jeremiah 29:11 – Discussion of God's plans for Israel's restoration.

Ezekiel 37 – Prophetic visions of restoration for Israel.

Commentaries on Acts

Darrell L. Bock: Acts (Baker Exegetical Commentary on the New Testament).

F. F. Bruce: The Book of Acts (The New International Commentary on the New Testament).

Eugene H. Peterson: The Message: The Book of Acts (The Message).

Theology of the Holy Spirit

Wayne Grudem: Systematic Theology: An Introduction to Biblical Doctrine – Chapter on the Holy Spirit.

Craig L. Blomberg: Jesus and the Gospels: An Introduction and Survey.

Church History

John Stott: The Spirit, the Church, and the World: The Message of Acts.

Historical Context

The Jewish Calendar – Its significance to Pentecost.

Bill T. Arnold and Bryan E. Beyer: Encountering the Old Testament: A Christian Survey.

Cultural Studies on the Early Church

N.T. Wright: Simply Jesus: A New Vision of Who He Was, What He Did, and Why He Matters.

Alister McGrath: Historical Theology: An Introduction to the History of Christian Thought.

Scholarly Articles and Journals

Various theological journals: "The Holy Spirit and the Birth of the Church: An Exegesis of Acts 2"; "The Inclusion of the Gentiles in Acts: Theological Implications."

Books on the Early Church and Missions

John Stott: The Spirit, the Church, and the World (discussion on the mission of the Church).

Richard A. Horsley: Paul and Empire: Religion and Power in Roman Imperial Society.

Additional Resources

Craig S. Keener: The Spirit in the Gospels and the Acts (focus on the work of the Spirit).

Christopher J. H. Wright: The Mission of God: Unlocking the Bible's Grand Narrative.

John Ortberg: The Life You've Always Wanted: Spiritual Disciplines for Ordinary People.

Theological and Scholarly References

John Walvoord: "The Rapture Question" – A comprehensive look at different Rapture views and theological implications.

Robert L. Thomas: Revelation 1-7: An Exegetical Commentary – Insights on the events during the Tribulation period.

Charles C. Ryrie: Basic Theology – A foundational understanding of eschatology.

J. Dwight Pentecost: Things to Come: A Study in Biblical Eschatology – Discusses the prophetic aspects of the end times.

Tim LaHaye and Jerry B. Jenkins: Left Behind series – Fictional works that popularize views on the Rapture and Tribulation.

Online Resources

Bible Gateway: For cross-referencing different translations.

The Bible Project: Videos on Acts and the Holy Spirit.

Made in United States
North Haven, CT
03 December 2024